DUCATI

160-450cc SINGLES • THROUGH 1974

SERVICE • REPAIR • MAINTENANCE

ERIC JORGENSEN
Editor

JEFF ROBINSON
Publisher

CLYMER PUBLICATIONS

World's largest publisher of books devoted exclusively to
automobiles and motorcycles.

12860 MUSCATINE STREET • P.O. BOX 20 • ARLETA, CALIFORNIA 91331

FIRST EDITION
First Printing July, 1974
Second Printing June, 1975
Third Printing November, 1977
Fourth Printing July, 1979

Printed in U.S.A.

ISBN: 0-89287-004-4

MTA
MEMBER

MIC
MOTORCYCLE INDUSTRY COUNCIL

CONTENTS

QUICK REFERENCE DATA

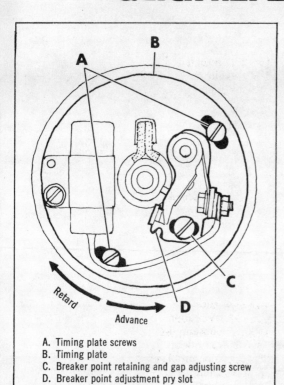

A. Timing plate screws
B. Timing plate
C. Breaker point retaining and gap adjusting screw
D. Breaker point adjustment pry slot

IDLE SPEED

160	1,100-1,300 rpm
250-450	1,000-1,200 rpm

CHASSIS ADJUSTMENTS

Clutch lever free play	1/16-1/8 in. (2-3mm)
Drive chain play	3/4-1 in. (20-25mm)
Brake pedal travel	3/4-1 in. (20-25mm)
Brake lever free play	1/16-1/8 in. (2-3mm)

REPLACEMENT BULBS

Headlight	GE 6867
Tail/stoplight	SAE 4117
Instruments	SAE 1262

ENGINE TUNE-UP

Spark Plugs	
Type (160)	NGK B8HS, Bosch W240T1, Champion L77JC
(250-450)	NGK B7HS, Bosch W225T1, Champion L81MC
Gap (all)	0.024 in. (0.1mm)
Valve Clearance (set cold)	
160, 250 Monza, 250 GT	0.012 in. (0.3mm) both valves
250 Mach I, 250 Scrambler, 250 Mark 3	0.010 in. (0.25mm) intake 0.016 in. (0.4mm) exhaust
350 (all)	0.012 in. (0.3mm) both valves
450 Mark 3, 450 Scrambler	0.002-0.004 in. (0.05-0.10mm) both valves
450 Desmo	0.004-0.006 in. (0.10-0.15mm) both valves
Breaker Point Gap	0.012-0.015 in. (0.3-0.4mm)
Static Ignition Timing (BTDC)	
160 Monza	21-23°
250 GT, Monza, Mach I	5-8°
250 Mark 3 (1963-1964)	38-41°
250 Mark 3 (1965-1966)	21-23°
250 Motocross (to engine No. 87.902)	38-41°
250 Motocross (from engine No. 87.903)	21-23°
350 Sebring	5-8°
450 Mark 3, Desmo, Scrambler	0°
450 Desmo-Cross-Special	7°

TIGHTENING TORQUES

Fastener Size in Millimeters		Torque Ft.-lb.	Torque Mkg
Bolt	Nut		
6	10	7.2	1.0
8	13-14	15	2.0
10	17	25-29	3.5-4.0
12	19	29-33	4.0-4.5
14	22	33-36	4.5-5.0
17-18	26-27	43-51	6.0-7.0
20	30	51-58	7.0-8.0
Spark plug		18-22	2.5-3.0

TIRES

	Front	Rear
Pressure (street)	30-32 psi*	30-32 psi*
Pressure (off-road)	26-28 psi	26-28 psi
Standard size		
160	2.75 x 16	3.25 x 16
250 GT	2.75 x 18	3.00 x 18
250 Mark 3, Mach I	2.50 x 18	2.75 x 18
250 Scrambler	3.00 x 19	3.50 x 19
	3.00 x 19	4.00 x 18
350-450	2.75 x 18	3.00 x 18

* Add 2 psi for sustained high speed riding.

RECOMMENDED LUBRICANTS AND FUEL

Fluid	Capacity	Classification	Temp. Range	Viscosity
Engine oil				
160	2.5 qt. (2.4 liter)	API SD, SE	Above 40°F	SAE 10W-40, SAE 40
		API SD, SE	Below 40°F	SAE 10W-40, SAE 30
250-450	2.25 qt. (2.1 liter)	API SD, SE	Above 40°F	SAE 10W-40, SAE 40
		API SD, SE	Below 40°F	SAE 10W-40, SAE 30
Fork oil				
160	5.2 oz. (150cc)	——	All	SAE 20W
250-450	3.5 oz. (110cc)	——	All	Hydraulic brake fluid DOT 3
Wheel bearings and all fittings	As required	NLG1 2 multi-purpose grease	All	90W
Cables	As required	WD40, graphite, or special cable lube	All	——
Gasoline				
160, 250 Monza	3.4 gal. (13 liter)	Regular	——	——
250 GT	4.5 gal. (17 liter)	Regular	——	——
250 Mk 3, Mach I	4.2 gal. (16 liter)	Regular	——	——
250 Scrambler	2.9 gal. (11 liter)	Premium	——	——
350-450	3.4 gal. (13 liter)	Premium	——	——

CHAPTER ONE

GENERAL INFORMATION

This book has been written to help owners of all Ducati single cylinder motorcycles. Specific service procedures are given for the most common models. The procedures are similar for other models not specifically mentioned in the text.

All Ducati engines are similar in design and use compatible components. The only differences will be in carburetion, ignition, number of transmission gears or bore and stroke dimensions. Even the 750cc twin, a limited production model, is nothing more than a pair of siamesed standard cylinders.

Procedures common to several different models are combined in one chapter, to avoid duplication. Read the following service hints to make the work as easy and pleasant as possible. Performing your own work can be an enjoyable and rewarding experience.

SERVICE HINTS

Most of the service procedures covered are straightforward and can be performed by anyone reasonably handy with tools. It is suggested, however, that you consider your own capabilities carefully before attempting any operation involving major disassembly of the engine.

Some operations, for example, require the use of a press. It would be wiser to have these performed by a shop equipped for such work, rather than to try to do the job yourself with makeshift equipment. Other procedures require precision measurements. Unless you have the skills and equipment required, it would be better to have a qualified repair shop make the measurements for you.

Repairs go much faster and easier if your machine is clean before you begin work. There are special cleaners for washing the engine and related parts. Just brush or spray on the cleaning solution, let it stand, then rinse it away with a garden hose. Clean all oily or greasy parts with cleaning solvent as you remove them.

Never use gasoline as a cleaning agent. It presents an extreme fire hazard. Be sure to work in a well-ventilated area when using cleaning solvent. Keep a fire extinguisher, rated for gasoline fires, handy in any case.

Special tools are required for some repair procedures. These may be purchased at a Ducati dealer (or borrowed if you're on good terms with the service department) or may be fabricated by a mechanic or machinist, often at considerable savings.

Much of the labor charge for repairs made by dealers is for the removal and disassembly of other parts to reach the defective unit. It is frequently possible to perform the preliminary operations yourself and then take the defective unit in to the dealer for repair at considerable savings.

Once you have decided to tackle the job yourself, read the entire section in this manual which pertains to it, making sure you have identified the proper one. Study the illustrations and text until you have a good idea of what is involved in completing the job satisfactorily. If special tools are required, make arrangements to get them before you start. It is frustrating and time-consuming to get partly into a job and then be unable to complete it.

Simple wiring checks are easily made at home; but knowledge of electronics is almost a necessity for performing tests with complicated electronic testing gear.

During disassembly of parts keep a few general cautions in mind. Force is rarely needed to get things apart. If parts are a tight fit, like a magneto on a crankshaft, there is usually a tool designed to separate them. Never use a screwdriver to pry apart parts with machined surfaces such as crankcase halves and valve covers. You'll mar the surfaces and end up with leaks.

Make diagrams wherever similar-appearing parts are found. For instance, case cover screws are often not the same length. You may *think* you can remember where everything came from — but mistakes are costly. There is also the possibility you may be sidetracked and not return to work for days or even weeks — in which interval, carefully laid out parts may have become disturbed.

Wiring should be tagged with masking tape and marked as each wire is removed. Again, don't rely on memory alone.

Clutch plates, wiring connections and brake shoes and drums should be kept clean and free of grease and oil.

When assembling parts, be sure all shims and washers are replaced exactly as they came out. Whenever a rotating part butts against a stationary part, look for a shim or washer. Use new gaskets if there is any doubt about the condition of old ones. Generally you should apply gasket cement to one mating surface only so the parts may be easily disassembled in the future. A thin coat of oil on gaskets helps them seal effectively.

Heavy grease can be used to hold small parts in place if they tend to fall out during assembly. However, keep grease and oil away from electrical components or brake shoes and drums.

High spots may be sanded off a piston with sandpaper, but emery cloth and oil do a much more professional job.

Carburetors are best cleaned by disassembling them and soaking the parts in a commercial carburetor cleaner. Never soak gaskets and rubber parts in these cleaners. Never use wire to clean out jets and air passages; they are easily damaged. Use compressed air to blow out the carburetor only if the float has been removed first.

A baby bottle makes a good measuring device for adding oil to forks and transmissions. Get one that is graduated in ounces and cubic centimeters.

Take your time and do the job right. Don't forget that a newly rebuilt motorcycle engine must be broken in the same as a new one. Keep rpm's within the limits given in your owner's manual when you get back on the road.

TOOLS

Tool Kit

Most models were equipped with fairly complete tool kits as they left the factories when new. The kit is located in a large compartment under the left side of the seat on street models and is supplied separately on all others.

These tools are satisfactory for most small jobs and roadside repairs in an emergency.

Shop Tools

For proper servicing, you will need an assortment of ordinary hand tools. As a minimum, these include:

1. Metric combination wrenches
2. Metric sockets
3. Plastic mallet
4. Small hammer
5. Snap ring pliers
6. Phillips screwdrivers

7. Pliers
8. Slot screwdrivers
9. Feeler gauges
10. Spark plug gauge
11. Spark plug wrench
12. Dial indicator

Special tools necessary will be shown in the chapters covering the particular repair in which they are used. See **Figures 1 and 2**.

Electrical system servicing requires a voltmeter, ohmmeter or other device for determining continuity, and a hydrometer for battery equipped machines.

EXPENDABLE SUPPLIES

Certain expendable supplies are also required. These include grease, oil, gasket cement, wiping rags, cleaning solvent, and distilled water. Ask your dealer for the special locking compounds, silicone lubricants, and commercial chain lube products which make motorcycle maintenance simpler and easier. Solvent is available at most service stations and distilled water for the battery is available at most supermarkets.

SAFETY FIRST

Professional motorcycle mechanics can work for years and never sustain a serious injury. If you observe a few rules of common sense and safety, you can enjoy many safe hours servicing your own machine. You could hurt yourself or damage the bike if you ignore these rules.

1. Never use gasoline as a cleaning solvent.

2. Never smoke or use a torch in the vicinity of flammable liquids such as cleaning solvent in open containers.

3. Never smoke or use a torch in an area where batteries are being charged. Highly explosive hydrogen gas is formed during the charging process.

4. If welding or brazing is required on the machine, remove the fuel tank to a safe distance, at least 50 feet away. Welding on gas tanks requires special safety procedures and must be performed only by someone skilled in the process.

5. Use the proper sized wrenches to avoid damage to nuts and injury to yourself.

6. When loosening a tight or stuck nut, be guided by what would happen if the wrench should slip. Protect yourself accordingly.

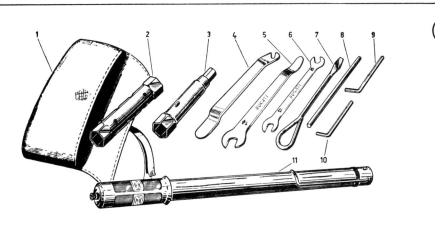

TYPICAL TOOL KIT

1. Tool bag
2. Double box wrench
3. Double box wrench
4. Tire lever
5. Hexagon wrench
6. Double hexagon wrench
7. Screwdriver
8. Leverage bar for box wrench
9. Allen wrench
10. Allen wrench
11. Tire pump

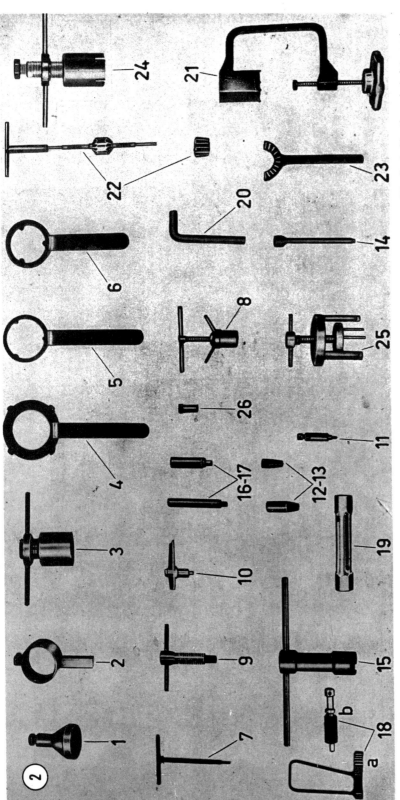

SPECIAL TOOLS

1. Flywheel magneto extractor
2. Piston grasp
3. Timing bearing holder bushing extractor
4. Crankshaft gear wrench
5. Clutch drum wrench
6. Countershaft sprocket wrench
7. Allen wrench
8. Valve seat clamps
9. Clutch-side cover extractor
10. Piston position indicator
11. Rocker pin extractor
12. Cone for fitting round or square sectioned spring rings
13. Cone for fitting circlip on gearshift mainshaft
14. Pin for orienting washers and brushes when fitting rocker pins
15. Timing shaft wrench
16. Pin for fitting and refitting gudgeon pins
17. Pin for fitting and refitting gudgeon pins
18a. For locking the mainshaft tapered gear (with cylinder head assembled)
18b. For locking the mainshaft tapered gear (with cylinder head disassembled)
19. Box wrench
20. Allen wrench
21. Clamp for assembling and disassembling valves with needle springs
22. Cone milling cutter and wrench.
23. Exhaust pipe clamping-ring wrench
24. Bearing extractor
25. Not available
26. Bushing for fitting advance cover

7. Keep your work area clean and uncluttered.

8. Wear safety goggles during all operations involving drilling, grinding, or use of a cold chisel.

9. Never use worn tools.

10. Keep a fire extinguisher handy and be sure it is rated for gasoline and electrical fires.

SERIAL NUMBERS

You must know the model serial number for the sake of registration and when ordering special parts. These identification numbers are located in the same general area on all Ducati models.

The engine number is located on the crankcase between the front motor mount and frame as shown in **Figure 3** (next page).

The frame number is stamped on the steering head down-tube on the right-hand side. This same number is repeated on the central frame tube under the seat (near the battery on street models).

These numbers can be permanently recorded by placing a sheet of paper over the imprinted area and rubbing with the side of a pencil. Some motor vehicle registration offices will accept such evidence in lieu of inspecting the bike in person.

LOCATION OF CONTROLS

Figures 4, 5 and 6 show the location of controls on the two types of Ducati motorcycles. The new rider should acquaint himself with these prior to riding for the first time.

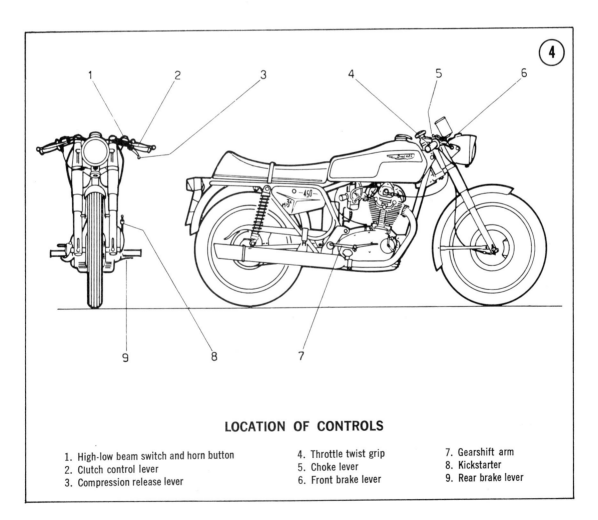

LOCATION OF CONTROLS

1. High-low beam switch and horn button
2. Clutch control lever
3. Compression release lever
4. Throttle twist grip
5. Choke lever
6. Front brake lever
7. Gearshift arm
8. Kickstarter
9. Rear brake lever

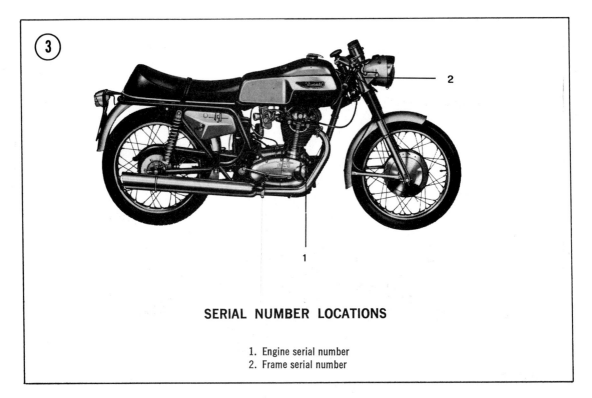

SERIAL NUMBER LOCATIONS

1. Engine serial number
2. Frame serial number

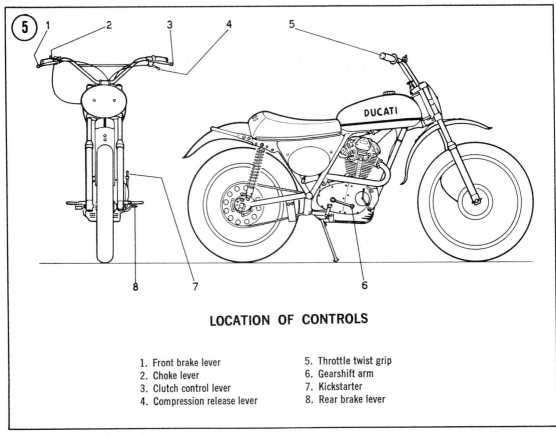

LOCATION OF CONTROLS

1. Front brake lever
2. Choke lever
3. Clutch control lever
4. Compression release lever
5. Throttle twist grip
6. Gearshift arm
7. Kickstarter
8. Rear brake lever

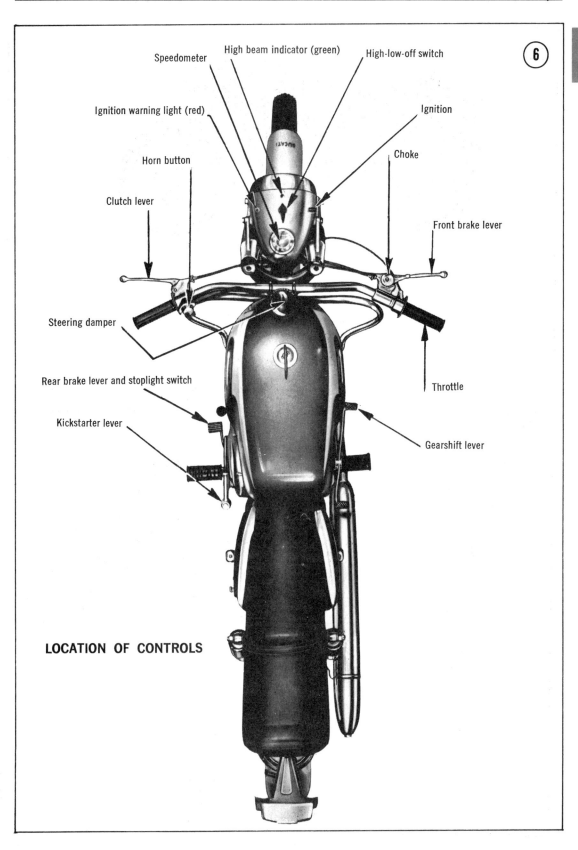

Speedometer

High beam indicator (green)

High-low-off switch

6

1

Ignition warning light (red)

Ignition

Horn button

Choke

Clutch lever

Front brake lever

Steering damper

Rear brake lever and stoplight switch

Throttle

Kickstarter lever

Gearshift lever

LOCATION OF CONTROLS

CHAPTER TWO

OVERHAUL AND LIMITS OF WEAR

Physical damage to components is usually obvious by visual inspection. Normal wear is not always so obvious and usually requires special measuring tools for detection.

This chapter indicates what to look for with visual and measured inspections. The tables indicate maximum and minimum tolerances allowed before replacement is needed. Never exceed these limits for any reason. The factory has been very careful and precise in compiling the specifications.

The tools needed should include vernier calipers, inside and outside micrometers, feeler gauges and a steel scale calibrated in tenths of an inch and millimeters.

Cylinder Head

1. Check all gasket mating surfaces. These should be smooth, clean, and free of scratches.

2. Check the valve guides for cracks, scoring or signs of wear. See **Table 1**.

3. Inspect valve stems and seating area.

4. See **Table 2** for the tension required by the valve springs. Place a weight equivalent to this amount on the springs. The springs should compress slightly and be parallel to the test bed base.

5. Rockers should be replaced if the hard-faced surface has been penetrated. If the wear is only slight, try polishing the surfaces. Refer to **Table 3** for limits.

Table 1   VALVE STEM-TO-GUIDE CLEARANCE

Model	Valve-Guide Bore ∅ = mm	Valve Stem ∅ = mm	Clearance min. & max. (mm)	Limits of wear (mm)
160 Monza Jr.	7.000	6.987	0.013	0.08
	7.022	6.965	0.057	
250, 350 and 450	8.000	7.987	0.013	0.08
	8.022	7.965	0.057	

Table 2   VALVE SPRING

Model	Spring Intake or Exhaust	P		L = mm	Limits of wear (mm)
		kg.	lb.		
160 Monza Junior	I	16 + 0.800	35.3	Parallel arms	
	E	16 + 0.800	35.3	Parallel arms	
250 Monza 250 Mark 3, 1964 250 SCR - GT, from eng. no. 87422	I	27 ± 0.650	59.5	Parallel arms	Arms converging
	E	22 + 1	48.5	Parallel arms	
250 GT to eng. no. 87421	I	22 + 1	48.5	Parallel arms	
	E	22 + 1	48.5	Parallel arms	
250 Mark 3, 1965-1966 250 Mach 1	I	27 ± 0.650	59.5	Parallel arms	
	E	27 ± 0.650	59.5	Parallel arms	
Does not apply to later models with Desmodromic valves (350-450)	—	—	—	—	—

Table 3   BUSHING/ROCKER CLEARANCE

Model	Rocker Bore ∅ = mm	Bushing Outside ∅ = mm	Max. Interference — Max. clearance + (mm)	Limits of wear (mm)
160 Monza Junior	11.000	11.012	— 0.012	0.04
	11.018	11.001	+ 0.017	
250, 350, and 450 series	13.000	13.012	— 0.012	0.04
	13.018	13.001	+ 0.017	

6. Refer to **Table 4** for limits of wear on rocker bushings and pins. Replace if needed.

7. The cam lobes should not be scored or wavy on the hard-faced surface. Check the lubrication holes to be sure they are clear.

8. Check the bevel drive gears for excessive side-play in the shaft, broken or chipped teeth, or worn mating surfaces.

Cylinder

1. Check the cylinder bore for signs of scoring and wear as indicated in **Tables 5A through 5E** and in relation to **Figure 1**.

2. The piston should be smooth on the circumference and the dome. Remove carbon deposits with a wire brush and polish with emery cloth.

3. Piston ring grooves should be clean and the

Table 4   ROCKER PIN AND BUSHING CLEARANCE

Model	Bushing Bore ∅ = mm	Rocker Pin ∅ = mm	Min. & max. clearance (mm)	Limits of wear (mm)
160 Monza Junior	8.013	8.010	0.003	0.05
	8.028	8.001	0.027	
250, 350, and 450 series	10.013	10.010	0.003	0.05
	10.028	10.001	0.027	

Table 5A   PISTON SIZES — 160 MONZA JUNIOR

Assembly	Cylinder C = mm		Piston D = mm		Max. clearance E = mm	Min. clearance E = mm	Limits of wear (mm)
Standard	A	61.00-61.01	B	60.92-60.91	0.10	0.08	0.15
	B	61.01-61.02	A	60.93-60.92			
1st rebore + 0.4	A	61.40-61.41	B	61.32-61.31			
	B	61.41-61.42	A	61.33-61.32			
2nd rebore + 0.6	A	61.60-61.61	B	61.52-61.51			
	B	61.61-61.62	A	61.53-61.52			
3rd rebore + 0.8	A	61.80-61.81	B	61.72-61.71			
	B	61.81-61.82	A	61.73-61.72			
4th rebore + 1	A	62.00-62.01	B	61.92-61.91			
	B	62.01-62.02	A	61.93-61.92			

Table 5B   PISTON SIZES — 250 MONZA, GT, SCRAMBLER

Assembly	Cylinder C = mm		Piston D = mm		Max. clearance E = mm	Min. clearance E = mm	Limits of wear (mm)
Standard	A	74.00-74.01	B	73.905-73.895	0.115	0.095	0.16
	B	74.01-74.02	A	73.915-73.905			
1st rebore + 0.4	A	74.40-74.41	B	74.305-74.295			
	B	74.41-74.42	A	74.315-74.305			
2nd rebore + 0.6	A	74.60-74.61	B	74.505-74.495			
	B	74.61-74.62	A	74.515-74.505			
3rd rebore + 0.8	A	74.80-74.81	B	74.705-74.695			
	B	74.81-74.82	A	74.715-74.705			
4th rebore + 1	A	75.00-75.01	B	74.905-74.895			
	B	75.01-75.02	A	74.915-74.905			

Table 5C   PISTON SIZES — 250 MARK 3, MACH 1

Assembly	Cylinder C = mm		Piston D = mm		Max. clearance E = mm	Min. clearance E = mm	Limits of wear (mm)
Standard	A	74.00-74.01	B	73.87-73.88			
	B	74.01-74.02	A	73.88-73.89			
1st rebore + 0.4	A	74.40-74.41	B	74.27-74.28			
	B	74.41-74.42	A	74.28-74.29			
2nd rebore + 0.6	A	74.60-74.61	B	74.47-74.48	0.14	0.12	0.19
	B	74.61-74.62	A	74.48-74.49			
3rd rebore + 0.8	A	74.80-74.81	B	74.67-74.68			
	B	74.81-74.82	A	74.68-74.69			
4th rebore + 1	A	75.00-75.01	B	74.87-74.88			
	B	75.01-75.02	A	74.88-74.89			

Table 5D   PISTON SIZES — 350 SEBRING

Assembly	Cylinder C = mm		Piston D = mm		Max. clearance E = mm	Min. clearance E = mm	Limits of wear (mm)
Standard	A	76.00-76.01	B	75.93-75.92			
	B	76.01-76.02	A	75.94-75.93			
1st rebore + 0.4	A	76.40-76.41	B	76.33-76.32			
	B	76.41-76.42	A	76.34-76.33			
2nd rebore + 0.6	A	76.60-76.61	B	76.53-76.52	0.09	0.07	0.14
	B	76.61-76.62	A	76.54-76.53			
3rd rebore + 0.8	A	77.00-77.01	B	76.93-76.92			
	B	76.81-76.82	A	76.74-76.73			
4th rebore + 1	A	77.00-77.01	B	76.93-16.92			
	B	77.01-77.02	A	76.94-76.93			

Table 5E   PISTON SIZES — 450cc MODELS

Assembly	Cylinder C = mm		Piston D = mm		Max. clearance E = mm	Min. clearance E = mm	Limits of wear (mm)
Standard	A	86.00-86.01	B	85.93-85.92			
	B	86.01-86.02	A	85.94-85.93			
1st rebore + 0.4	A	86.40-86.41	B	86.33-86.32			
	B	86.41-86.42	A	86.34-86.33			
2nd rebore + 0.6	A	86.60-86.61	B	86.53-86.52	0.09	0.07	0.14
	B	86.61-86.62	A	86.54-86.53			
3rd rebore + 0.8	A	86.80-86.81	B	86.73-86.72			
	B	86.81-86.82	A	86.74-86.73			
4th rebore + 1	A	87.00-87.01	B	86.93-86.92			
	B	87.01-87.02	A	86.94-86.93			

NOTE: A and B are classes of cylinders and pistons.

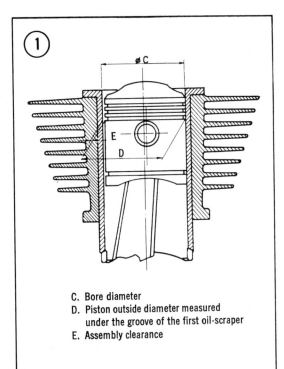

C. Bore diameter
D. Piston outside diameter measured under the groove of the first oil-scraper
E. Assembly clearance

holes under the scraper ring should be clear.

4. Check the limit for the rings in **Table 6** and **Figure 2**. Replace with the next larger over-bore size if needed. When new rings are installed, refer to the Tables 5A through 5E for correct cylinder rebore dimensions. A shop will have to match the piston and rings to the cylinder. It's impossible to perform this operation without the proper, expensive boring equipment. Refer to **Table 7** and **Figure 3** (page 14) for axial clearance of the rings.

5. The wrist pin must be a snug fit in the connecting rod bushing and a press fit in the piston. See **Table 8** and **Figure 4** (page 15).

Crankshaft and Connecting Rod

1. The bushing must be a press fit in the connecting rod bottom end. Replace with the next size larger outer diameter.

2. Make sure the bushing and crankshaft are parallel.

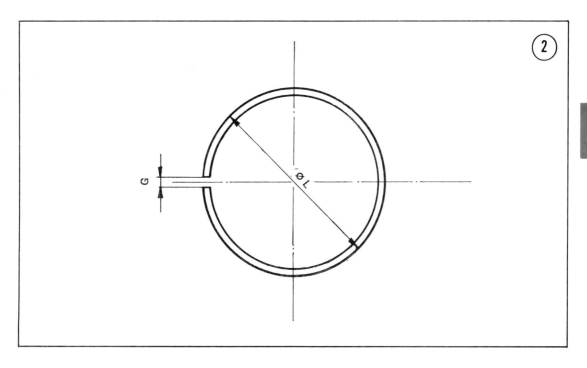

Table 6   PISTON RING END GAP

Model	O. D. of piston ring or oil-scraper in working position L = mm	Gap G = mm	Limits of wear (mm)
160 Monza Junior	61.00-61.02	0.15-0.30	0.80
250 Monza, GT, SCR	74.00-74.02	0.30-0.45	1.00
250 Mark 3, Mach 1	74.00-74.02	0.25-0.40	1.00
350 Sebring	76.00-76.02	0.30-0.45	1.00
450 Series	86.00-86.02	0.30-0.45	1.00

3. End-play and side clearance between the rod and crank pin is critical. Check **Tables 9 and 10** and **Figures 5 and 6** (pages 16-17).

4. Refer to **Table 11** and **Figure 7** (page 18) for clearance between the wrist pin and the connecting rod bushing.

5. Check the shaft bushing in the timing cover. The limits are .4775/.4736 inch (12.127/ 12.027mm).

Crankcase and Covers

Check:

1. Cover
2. Gasket mating surfaces
3. Bearings
4. Bushings
5. Oil seals
6. Oil tubes
7. Oil sump and filter

Clutch

Check:

1. Profile and wear of teeth.
2. Clutch driving plate slots.
3. Bearings.
4. Clutch plates for scoring, warpage or wear. Original plate thickness is 1.036 in. (27.0mm).

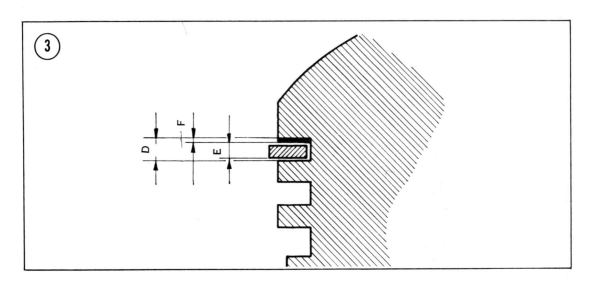

Table 7   **PISTON RING AXIAL CLEARANCE**

Model	1st & 2nd Piston rings E = mm	Oil scraper piston E = mm	Piston seat D = mm	Min. & Max. allowance F = mm	Limits of wear (mm)
160 Monza Junior	1.500	—	1.520	0.020	0.10
	1.488	—	1.540	0.052	
	—	2.500	3.520	0.020	
	—	2.488	3.540	0.052	
250 Monza	1.990	—	2.000	0.010	0.10
250 GT	1.978	—	2.020	0.042	
	—	2.490	2.500	0.010	
250 Motocross	—	2.478	2.520	0.042	
250 Mark 3, 1964	1.490	—	1.500	0.010	0.10
	1.478	—	1.520	0.042	
	—	2.990	3.000	0.010	
	—	2.978	3.020	0.042	
250 Mark 3, 1965-1966	1.490	—	1.510	0.020	0.10
	1.478	—	1.530	0.052	
250 Mach 1	—	2.990	3.010	0.020	
	—	2.978	3.030	0.052	
350 Sebring	1.490	—	1.510	0.020	0.10
	1.478	—	1.530	0.052	
	—	3.990	4.010	0.020	
	—	3.978	4.030	0.052	
450 Series	1.490	—	1.510	0.020	0.10
	1.478	—	1.530	0.052	
	—	3.990	4.010	0.020	
	—	3.978	4.030	0.052	

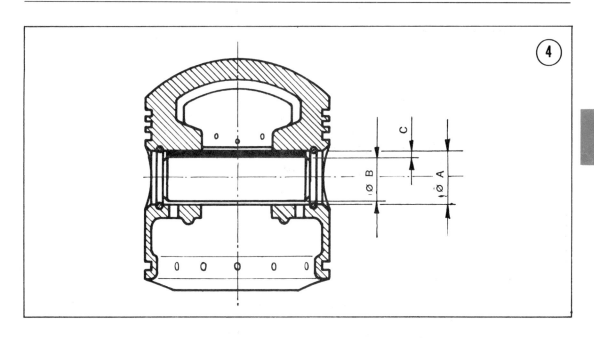

Table 8   PISTON/WRIST PIN INTERFERENCE AND CLEARANCE

160 Monza Junior				
Assembly	Piston ∅ A = mm	Piston Pin ∅ B = mm	Clearance + Interference — C = mm max.	Limits of wear (mm)
Standard	16.003	15.995	+ 0.008	
	15.997	16.000	— 0.003	
1st wrist pin oversize + 0.010	16.013	16.005	+ 0.008	
	16.007	16.010	— 0.003	
2nd wrist pin oversize + 0.015	16.018	16.010	+ 0.008	0.05
	16.012	16.015	— 0.003	
3rd wrist pin oversize + 0.020	16.023	16.015	+ 0.008	
	16.017	16.020	— 0.003	
250, 350, and 450 Series				
Assembly	Piston ∅ A = mm	Piston Pin ∅ B = mm	Clearance + Interference — C = mm max.	Limits of wear (mm)
Standard	18.003	17.995	+ 0.008	
	17.997	18.000	— 0.003	
1st wrist pin oversize + 0.010	18.013	18.005	+ 0.008	
	18.007	18.010	— 0.003	
2nd wrist pin oversize + 0.015	18.018	18.010	+ 0.008	0.05
	18.012	18.015	— 0.003	
3rd wrist pin oversize + 0.020	18.023	18.015	+ 0.008	
	18.017	18.020	— 0.003	

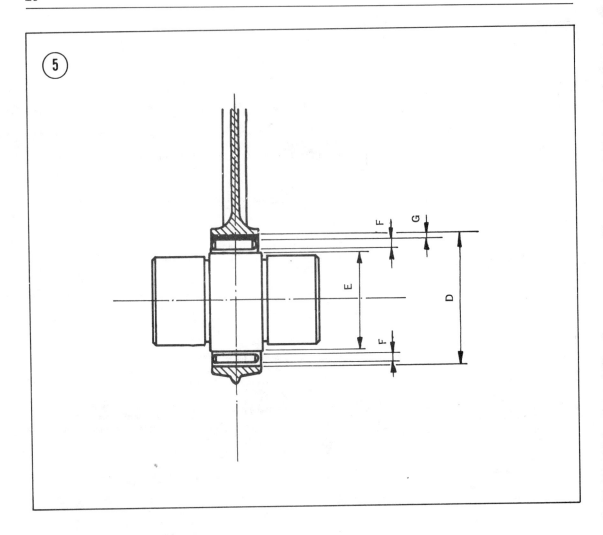

Table 9   CONNECTING ROD BIG END AND CRANK PIN TOLERANCE

160 Monza Junior				
Connecting Rod Big End D = mm	Crank Pin E = mm	Roller F = mm	Clearance min. and max. G = mm	Limits of wear (mm)
34.000 34.002	27.995 27.993	3.000 2.998	0.005 0.013	0.03

250, 350, and 450 Series				
Class	Connecting Rod Big End D = mm	Crank Pin E = mm	Roller F = mm	Interference — Clearance + G = mm max.	Limits of wear (mm)
A	39.000	32.006	3.500	— 0.006	0.03
A	39.010	32.000	3.498	+ 0.014	
B	38.994	32.000	3.500	— 0.006	0.03
B	39.000	31.990	3.498	+ 0.014	

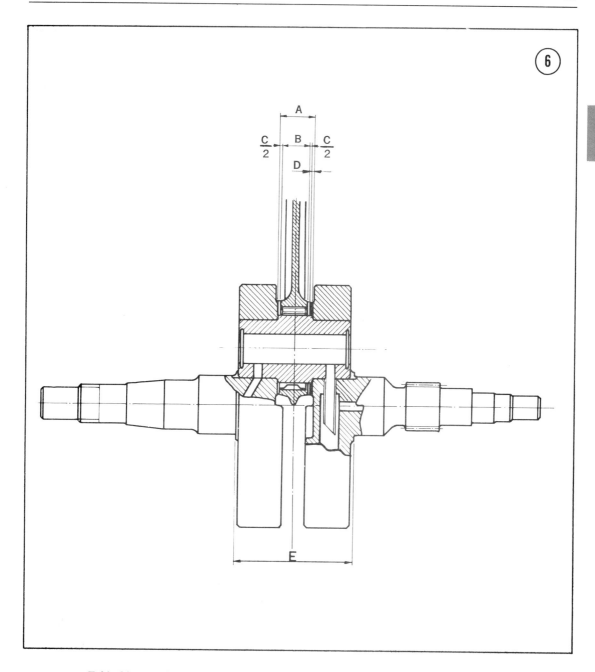

Table 10   CONNECTING ROD BIG END AND CRANK PIN AXIAL TOLERANCE

Model	Crank Pin A = mm	Connecting Rod Big End B = mm	Thrust Washers C = mm	Clearance min. & max. D = mm	Limits of wear (mm)
160 Monza Jr.	19.100	16.950	2.000	0.150	0.60
	19.150	16.907	1.820	0.423	
250, 350, and 450	20.100	17.950	2.000	0.150	0.60
	20.150	17.907	1.820	0.423	

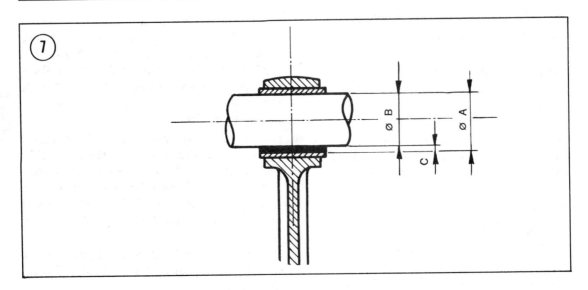

Table 11   WRIST PIN/CONNECTING ROD CLEARANCE

160 Monza Junior				
Assembly	**Connecting rod small end bushing ø A = mm**	**Wrist pin ø B = mm**	**Clearance min. & max. C = mm**	**Limits of wear (mm)**
Standard	16.005	16.000	0.005	
	16.023	15.995	0.028	
1st wrist pin oversize + 0.010	16.015	16.010	0.005	
	16.033	16.005	0.028	0.05
2nd wrist pin oversize + 0.015	16.020	16.015	0.005	
	16.038	16.010	0.028	
3rd wrist pin oversize + 0.020	16.025	16.020	0.005	
	16.043	16.015	0.028	
250, 350, and 450cc Models				
Assembly	**Connecting rod small end bushing ø A = mm**	**Wrist pin ø B = mm**	**Clearance min. & max. C = mm**	**Limits of wear (mm)**
Standard	18.000	18.000	0.000	
	18.018	17.995	0.023	
1st wrist pin oversize + 0.010	18.010	18.010	0.000	
	18.028	18.005	0.023	0.03
2nd wrist pin oversize + 0.015	18.015	18.015	0.000	
	18.033	18.010	0.023	
3rd wrist pin oversize + 0.020	18.020	18.020	0.000	
	18.038	18.015	0.023	

The plates may wear to .984 in. (25mm) but no less before replacing.

5. The steel plates won't wear out, but should be replaced if scored or warped.

6. Use the steel scale and check the flatness of the pressure plate.

7. The clutch springs, when new, are supposed to be 1.183 in. (30.4mm) long. A weight of 37 pounds should compress the spring to 25/32 in. (20mm). A 5% leeway is permissible.

Oil Pump

1. Check the gear teeth.

2. The limits of wear for the two gear recesses are .748/.945 in. (19.0/19.5mm) in diameter and .354/.359 in. (9.00/9.12mm) deep.

3 Clearance between the gear and pin should be no more than .002 in. (0.05mm).

4. The maximum clearance between the driving gear and body bushing should be no more than .0016 in. (0.04mm).

Starter and Gearbox

1. Check the bearings.

2. Clearance between the shafts and bushings should be no more than .004 in. (0.10mm).

3. The fork control guides are .3185 in. (8.090mm) wide when new and should be no less than .3145 in. (7.990mm) when worn.

4. Check the gears for obvious signs of wear.

5. The gearbox mainshaft should be perfectly straight for smooth operation and longevity. Place the shaft in a pair of "vee" blocks and check the straightness with a dial indicator. Run-out should be no more than .002 in. (0.05mm). The shaft may be straightened in a press by a competent mechanic.

6. The starter bushing is located in the clutch side of the crankcase and is .5914 in. (15.027 mm) when new. It should be no more than .5954 in. (15.127mm) for replacement. The bushing in the cover is .7095 in. (18.018mm) when new and should not exceed .7135 in. (18.118mm).

7. The bushing in the starter/first gear is .6701 in. (17.034mm) and should not exceed .6741 in. (17.134mm).

Distributor

1. Check the drive gear.

2. The bushing is .5914 in. (15.027mm) when new and should not exceed .5954 in. (15.127 mm) when worn.

3. Replace the O-ring if it appears cracked or if leaks develop.

Specifications

Chapter Ten gives the specifications of the more popular Ducati models.

Critical dimensions are listed under specific headings in the section on *Limits of Wear*.

CHAPTER THREE

ELECTRICAL SYSTEM

This chapter covers operating principles and troubleshooting techniques for ignition, charging, and lighting systems. Most motorcycle manufacturers use either a generator (dynamo) or flywheel magneto system to produce electricity.

The efficiency of the generator system depends on the perfect functioning of such easily damaged components as the commutator, brushes, and regulator.

The flywheel magneto system is simple in construction, sturdy, and produces a hot spark for ignition. The disadvantage is varying intensity of the lights in relation to engine rpm.

Ducati utilizes a completely rectified magneto system which combines the advantages of magneto and generator systems while minimizing the problems.

Magneto Operation

Figure 1 illustrates a simplified magneto system of the type used by Ducati. Magnets move past an ignition source coil, as the flywheel rotates, inducing current within the coil. Breaker points are opened by a cam, attached to the crankshaft, just as the piston reaches firing position. As the points open, energy is transferred from the source coil to the ignition coil, a form of transformer, where it is stepped up to the high voltage required to jump the spark plug

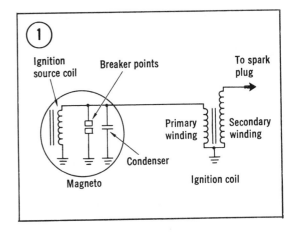

gap for ignition. This process recurs once every second revolution or as much as 3,500 times a minute. It is essential that all components are functioning properly and timing is correct for maximum engine efficiency at these speeds.

Magneto Applications

Three types of flywheel magneto alternators are used by Ducati.

6V-40W   This unit contains a lighting coil and ignition source coil. It is used on all models not utilizing a battery for lights including the 250 Mark 3 and Scrambler until engine number 92171 (**Figure 2**).

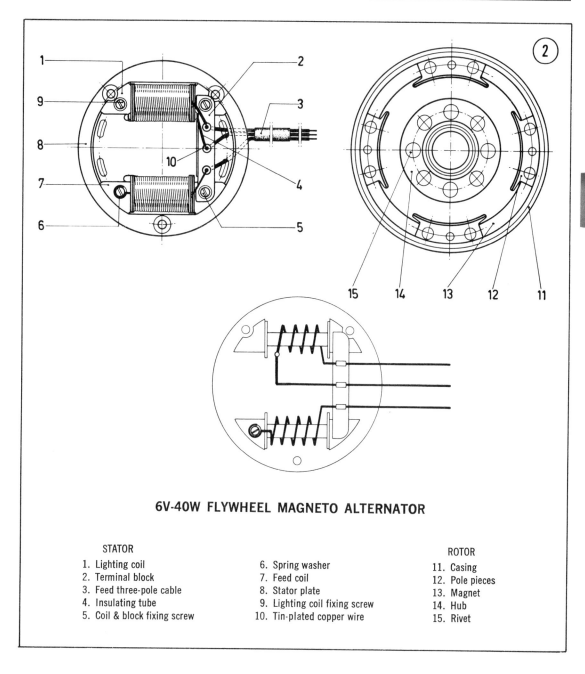

6V-40W FLYWHEEL MAGNETO ALTERNATOR

STATOR		ROTOR
1. Lighting coil	6. Spring washer	11. Casing
2. Terminal block	7. Feed coil	12. Pole pieces
3. Feed three-pole cable	8. Stator plate	13. Magnet
4. Insulating tube	9. Lighting coil fixing screw	14. Hub
5. Coil & block fixing screw	10. Tin-plated copper wire	15. Rivet

6V-60W This unit contains four charging coils to supply ignition voltage and to recharge the battery for lighting. It is used on the 250 Monza, 250 GT, 250 Mach 1, and 350 Sebring (**Figure 3**).

6V-28W This unit is similar to *6V-40W* and is used on the 160 Monza Jr. and 250 Scrambler.

Battery

The battery stores electrical energy until needed to power the lights and horn. On some bikes, equipped with generators, the battery is also used for ignition. Fortunately all Ducati bikes can be started with a dead battery because of the ignition coils in the magneto.

Battery neglect is the most frequent cause of problems with motorcycle electrical systems. A

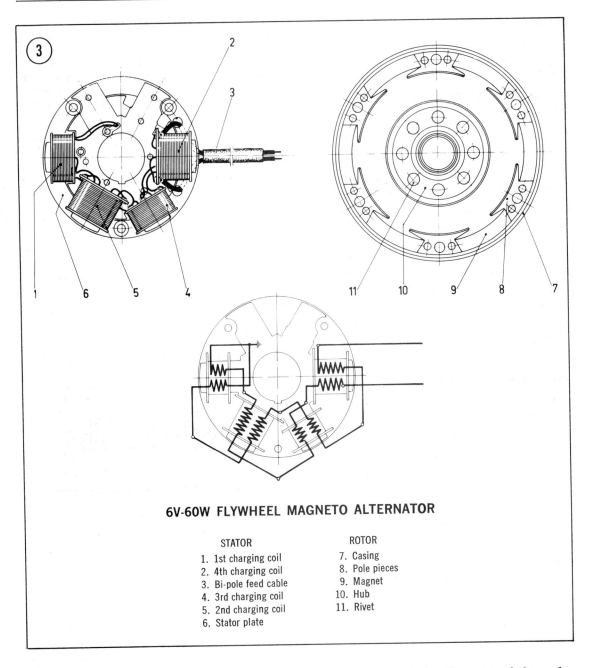

6V-60W FLYWHEEL MAGNETO ALTERNATOR

STATOR	ROTOR
1. 1st charging coil	7. Casing
2. 4th charging coil	8. Pole pieces
3. Bi-pole feed cable	9. Magnet
4. 3rd charging coil	10. Hub
5. 2nd charging coil	11. Rivet
6. Stator plate	

frequent check of fluid levels and for external signs of damage will prolong battery life.

Fill the battery to the "fill" mark as often as needed with distilled water. *Never* use tap water except in extreme emergencies. The minerals in tap water build up over a period of time as the water evaporates causing irreparable damage to the plates. Distilled water can be purchased in any market.

Never allow the battery to discharge com-pletely or to remain in a low state of charge for any length of time or damage will result. Keep the vent plugs tightened and replace is necessary.

Clean the terminals and connections by re-moving oxides and protect with a thin coat of Vaseline or silicone spray.

If the bike is to be unused for a long period of time, remove the battery and store in a cool, dry place. Check the fluid levels once a month, or more often in dry climates.

Recharging

Charge the battery once a month with a common "trickle" style charger even if the bike is in constant use. This is cheap insurance against ruining a good battery. Remove the battery from the frame prior to charging. The charge rate should be 1/10th the amperage capacity over a period of 10 hours. Be sure to hook up the "plus" lead from the charger to the "plus" terminal of the battery. Check the temperature of the electrolyte with a thermometer to make sure it doesn't exceed 122°F (50°C). If this figure is exceeded, reduce the charge rate or disconnect until the temperature drops to 104°F (40°C).

Charging must continue until the electrolyte density is constant for three consecutive readings made at one hour intervals or until the battery registers 8.1 volts. Simple automotive-type hydrometers may be purchased at motorcycle shops to check electrolyte density.

Installing a New Battery

If the battery won't hold a charge, it must be replaced. Two types of battery are used in the various models. These are:

SAFA 3L3- 13.5 Ah-6V   This high amperage unit is used to supply power for the lighting equipment of the 250 Monza, 250 GT, 250 Mach 1, 350 Sebring and 450 series. Charge rate is 1.35 amps.

SAFA 3IL3- 7 Ah-6V   Used for the lesser energy requirements of the 160 Monza Jr. and 250 Scrambler from engine number 92172. Charge rate is .7 amps.

Charging a New Battery

The battery must be charged with fresh sulphuric acid, pure enough to qualify for use in batteries, diluted with distilled water. The density at 59°F (15°C) is indicated in **Table 1**.

The specific gravity of electrolyte varies with temperature so a correction factor is needed for all but ideal conditions. Add or subtract 0.004 to the indicated specific gravity for every ten degrees over or under 59°F.

Table 1   ELECTROLYTE DENSITY

Ambient Conditions	Electrolyte Density		Electrolyte max. temperature during charge
	Filling	Charged	
Temperate climate	1.28 1.29	1.27 1.28	122° F 50° C
Tropical climate	1.21 1.22	1.20 1.21	140° F 60° C

The level of electrolyte in the cells must be at the top level of the anti-splash gauze as in **Figure 4**. Let the battery rest and cool for two hours after filling.

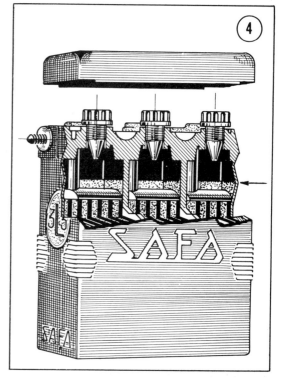

Prior to recharging, recheck the electrolyte level. The fluid is partially absorbed by the separators and plates. Bring the level up by adding more sulphuric acid. This is the only time the battery will be filled with acid. Always use distilled water for subsequent fillings. Measure the level with ebonite or glass sticks only. Any other substance could contaminate the cells.

Charge the battery for a total of 48 hours in 8 hour increments. Allow enough time between segments for the battery to cool. Continual charging could overheat the plates causing warpage, reduced efficiency, and life. The charge rate should be 1/10th of the rated amperage of the battery (.7 for a 7 Ah battery). Voltage at the end of the charge time should be 2.7 volts for each cell and 8.1 volts for a 3-cell unit.

Rectifier

The rectifier is a current static regulator unit rated at 6 volts and 10 amps. It converts the magneto's alternating current into direct current to be stored in the battery. It is also used to regulate the charging rate of the battery to prevent damage from over-charging and heat.

The red lamp, in the instrument cluster, is an indicator of the regulated charging condition. A mild glow at low rpm is normal and indicates that charging is not taking place. A constant bright glow at high rpm or cruising speeds indicates that the battery is not charging and something is wrong within the system. Try to determine the problem immediately to avoid damage to the rest of the electrical system.

Checking the Regulator (Static)

1. Remove the fuse cover and check the 15A fuses for continuity (Figure 22, Nos. 7, 13, and 14). Usually, an open circuit in the fuse is obvious by visual inspection. The interior of the glass will be black and the element will be shriveled. In rare instances, the connection may have been broken from vibration. A positive check can be made with a circuit tester made of a flashlight bulb and battery. Place the fuse in line with the bulb and battery. If the bulb does not light, replace the fuse.

2. To check the diodes rectifying the power, insert ohmmeter or circuit tester probes between the red and yellow No. 1 leads (**Figure 5**). You will have continuity with the lamp lighted or insulation with the lamp out. Reverse the probes from red to yellow No. 1 or vice versa. The situation should reverse. If there is continuity in both cases, the No. 1 diode is short-circuited. Insulation in both cases indicates a burned-out diode.

Repeat the test for diode No. 2 with the same red lead and yellow lead No. 2.

3. To check the diodes rectifying the warning light circuit, insert ohmmeter or circuit tester probes between the brown lead and yellow No. 1. Check for continuity (light on) or insulation (light off). Continuity in both instances indicates a short. Insulation in both instances indicates a burned-out diode.

Hook up an ohmmeter between the brown and green take-off points. The resistance should read 28 ohms.

4. Insert the ohmmeter between the red and grey take-off points. Continuity indicates good coil windings.

5. Insert the ohmmeter probes between the regulator support plates (ground) and take-off points, yellow No. 1, yellow No. 2, grey, green, brown, and red. These circuits should be insulated.

6. Replace regulator if any of the 5 previous steps aren't as they should be. Never attempt repairs of the regulator at home. The unit is carefully designed and calibrated at the factory. Incompetent repair could cause serious and costly damage to the electrical system.

Checking the Regulator (Operative)

1. Check the wiring harness for obvious signs of shorting (melted or blackened wiring) or open circuits, especially the parts regarding the alternator, regulator, and battery.

2. Disconnect the positive (+) cable from the battery terminal. Hook a direct current, .15 amp capacity, centered zero, ammeter in line with this circuit.

3. Now connect a DC voltmeter of 8 to 10 volt capacity between the positive (+) and negative (−) terminals of the battery. A reading of at least 4V is needed to activate the regulator for current output.

4. Start the engine and gradually increase speed to 6,000 rpm.

5. To check the maximum output, switch on the lights and check the meters. The voltage should be less than 7V and amperage should be approximately 5 amps.

6. To check the minimum output, turn off the lights and again check the meters. The battery

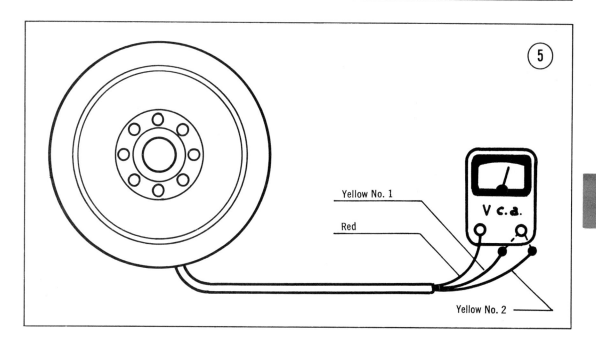

Yellow No. 1

Red

Yellow No. 2

voltage should gradually increase to the regulated value of approximately 5V.

7. Charging current should gradually decrease to 1 amp when the battery is again fully charged.

8. Maximum or zero current output is an indication that the regulator is defective and should be replaced. Figures lower than those mentioned in Step 5 indicate possible malfunctioning of the alternator and should be checked separately.

Checking the Alternator

1. Disconnect the 3 cables of the alternator from the terminal block.

2. Make sure the red cable (headlight) and ground wire are connected in circuit.

3. Check to be sure the white (stoplight) and yellow cables are connected in circuit.

4. If one or both circuits are not complete, remove the alternator and check the connections and solder joints in the stator. An ohmmeter, scale set at 1,000 ohms, should be used for these checks.

Alternator Rotor

1. Start the engine and run at 3,000 rpm.

2. Turn on the headlight and connect a voltmeter between the red power cable and ground. The reading should be about 5.5 volts DC.

3. Repeat the process for the taillight lead and ground. The results should also be 5.5 volts DC.

4. If a higher engine speed is needed to achieve this figure, the rotor will have to be remagnetized or, more likely, replaced.

Coil

The high tension coil converts low voltage to the high output required to jump the spark plug gap for ignition. In all battery equipped bikes, the coil is in direct current. On magneto fired bikes it is in AC.

The only maintenance required is that of keeping the connections clean and tight, and occasionally checking to see that the coil is mounted properly. If the proper operation is doubtful, use the following methods to check its condition.

1. Measure the resistance between the primary wire and ground with an ohmmeter. The resistance should be approximately one ohm. Measure the resistance between the secondary winding and ground. The figure should be 3,000 ohms.

3. If the meter indicated an open circuit in Step 2, try cutting the end off of the high voltage wire. Reattach the spark plug wire and recheck the resistance. If a reading can be made now, the trouble was at the connection.

4. If all tests prove correct, but operation is still doubtful, replace the defective unit with one known to be in functioning condition as a test.

Condenser

The condenser (capacitor) is a sealed unit and requires no maintenance. Be sure the connections are clean and tight.

The only possible proper test is to measure the resistance of the insulation with an ohmmeter. This value should be at least 5 megohms. A make-do test is to charge the capacitor by hooking the leads, or case and lead, to a 6V battery. After a few seconds, touch the leads together, or lead to case, and check for a spark, as shown in **Figure 6**. A damaged capacitor won't store electricity or spark.

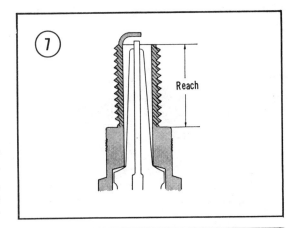

Reach

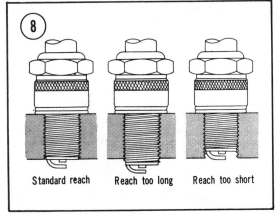

Standard reach   Reach too long   Reach too short

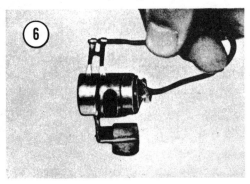

Spark Plug

Ducati motorcycles come equipped with the plug best suited for most riding situations. The standard plug should be replaced only with the same plug or its equivalent from another manufacturer. A hotter plug could cause excessive heat and subsequent damage to the piston. A colder plug would load up too easily during prolonged low-speed operation.

The reach (length) of a plug is also important. A longer than normal plug could interfere with the valves and piston causing permanent and severe damage. Refer to **Figures 7 and 8**.

A quick and simple test can be made to determine if the plug is correct for your type of riding. Accelerate hard through the gears and maintain a high, steady speed. Shut the throttle off, and kill the engine at the same time, allowing the bike to slow, out of gear. Don't allow the engine to slow the bike. Remove the plug and check the

condition of the electrode area. A spark plug of the correct heat range, with the engine in a proper state of tune, will appear light tan.

If the insulator is white or burned, the plug is too hot and should be replaced with a colder one. Also check the setting of the carburetor for it may be too lean. See **Figure 9**.

A too cold plug will have sooty deposits ranging in color from dark brown to black. Replace with a hotter plug and check for too rich carburetion or evidence of oil blow-by at the piston rings.

Remove and clean the spark plug at least once every 1,000 miles of riding. Electrode gap should be measured with a round feeler gauge and set at 0.013 to 0.017 inch as shown in **Figure 10** (page 28). Most riders prefer to replace the plugs at regular intervals because of the low cost.

Often, heat and corrosion can cause the plug to bind in the head making removal difficult. Don't use force; the head can easily be damaged.

(9)

3

Normal plug appearance noted by the brown to grayish-tan deposits and slight electrode wear. This plug indicates the correct plug heat range and proper air fuel ratio.

Red, brown, yellow and white coatings caused by fuel and oil additives. These deposits are not harmful if they remain in a powdery form.

Carbon fouling distinguished by dry, fluffy black carbon deposits which may be caused by an over-rich air/fuel mixture, excessive hand choking, clogged air filter or excessive idling.

Shiny yellow glaze on insulator cone is caused when the powdery deposits from fuel and oil additives melt. Melting occurs during hard acceleration after prolonged idling. This glaze conducts electricity and shorts out the plug.

Oil fouling indicated by wet, oily deposits caused by oil pumping past worn rings or down the intake valve guides. A hotter plug temporarily reduces oil deposits, but a plug that is too hot leads to pre-ignition and possible engine damage.

Overheated plug indicated by burned or blistered insulator tip and badly worn electrodes. This condition may be caused by pre-ignition, cooling system defects, lean air/fuel ratios, low octane fuel or over advanced ignition timing.

Spark plug condition photos courtesy of AC Spark Plug Division, General Motors Corporation.

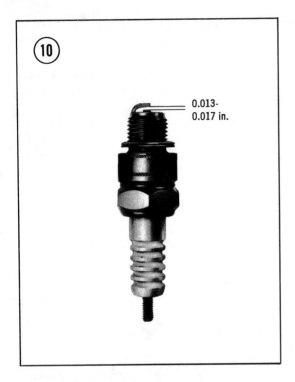

0.013-
0.017 in.

Apply penetrating oil to the base of the plug and allow it to work into the threads. Clean the seating area after removal and apply graphite to the threads to simplify future removal. Always use a new gasket. Run the plug in finger-tight and tighten one-quarter of a turn more with a wrench. Further tightening will only flatten the gasket and cause binding.

Mototrans Electronic Ignition

Some of the later models of Ducati are available with an electronic ignition system which eliminates breaker points, cams, and other moving parts. Spark plug fouling is eliminated because of the extremely fast rise time of the generated high voltage. Starting is simplified, power is increased, emissions are diminished, and the engine generally lasts longer thanks to this system.

Figure 11 is a wiring diagram of the typical unit. Alternating current is induced into coil No. 1 by the rotor of the rotating magneto. The current is rectified by the zener diode No. 2 and fed into condenser No. 3 to charge it with direct current. A thyristor (SCR), No. 4, blocks passage of current and prevents the condenser from discharging. Coil No. 6 picks up current from the rotor producing a signal for the thyristor to release current to the ignition coil No. 7. The coil steps up voltage to jump the gap at the spark plug No. 8. Resistor No. 5 acts as a limiter to the amount of current flow. These functions all take place within a fraction of a second. A normal ignition system with mechanical points is limited in function at high rpm.

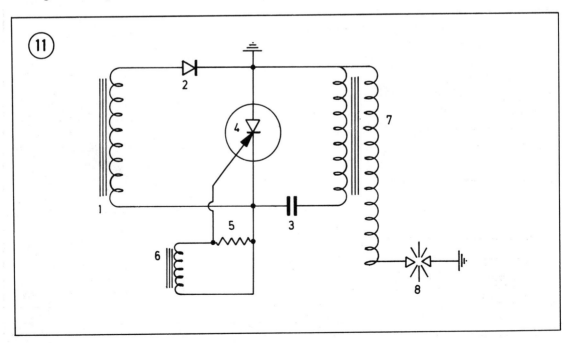

Electronic Ignition Timing

Since there are no moving parts in the system, maintenance is simple. Occasionaly check all connections for tightness and corrosion. Be sure the mounting bracket makes good contact with the frame to ground current. Check continuity between the case and the frame with an ohmmeter. Lack of a good ground could cause a malfunction.

Correct timing can be effected by aligning the marks in the top of the casing in the right side of the engine. The marks are aligned for maximum advance and should be correct for most conditions. At this point, the rotor and stator are "in phase". Subsequent marks are indicated for ten degrees of rotation of the crank. Timing may be altered by loosening the stator plate retaining screws and rotating the plate. Exact timing can only be performed with the aid of a strobe light. Follow the procedure outlined for conventional point systems except rotate the stator plate instead of the contact breaker point plate to alter timing. Rotate the plate clockwise to advance timing and counterclockwise to retard.

Ignition Timing, Conventional Breaker Points and Battery

Timing should be checked after the first 500 miles of operation and every 1,000 miles thereafter. Either a degree wheel or a strobe light are needed for accurate adjustment.

1. Remove the point cover on the right side of the engine case.

2. Check the condition of the contact breaker points as shown in **Figure 12**. The points should be clean, unburned and should make parallel contact. The points may be cleaned with a business card drawn between the contacts when closed or dressed with a special stone if not badly pitted. It's generally a better idea to use new points.

3. Remove the threaded plug, which is located at the driveshaft level, and install a degree wheel as shown in **Figure 13**.

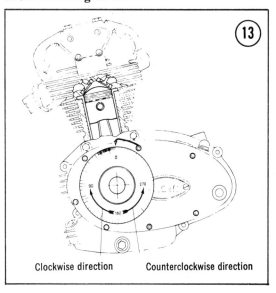

Clockwise direction   Counterclockwise direction

4. Hook up a light to the points as shown in **Figure 14**.

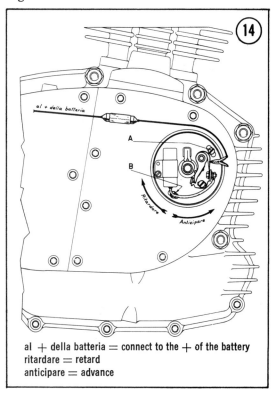

al + della batteria = connect to the + of the battery
ritardare = retard
anticipare = advance

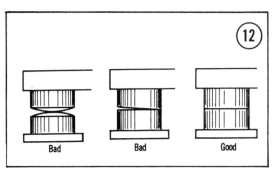

Bad   Bad   Good

5. Place an indicator on one of the case screws as shown in Figure 13.

6. Remove the spark plug and rotate the engine, with your finger in the plug hole, until compression can be felt. Bring the piston around to TDC (top dead center). A dial indicator in the spark plug hole will indicate when the piston has reached the top of its stroke. Align the pointer with the mark "0" on the degree wheel.

7. Rotate the driveshaft clockwise approximately a quarter of a turn. The lamp should come on at this point.

8. Rotate the crankshaft counterclockwise until the lamp just goes out, and stop. At this point the pointer should indicate a number on the degree wheel. See **Table 2** for correct setting.

9. Adjust the point gap to .012-.015 inches (0.3-0.4mm). See **Figure 15,** and recheck the settings established in Steps 7 and 8.

10. If the setting isn't accurate, loosen the point plate and rotate until the lamp does go out at the correct setting. Repeat the tests in previous steps as a precaution.

11. Lubricate the felt block with a single drop of light oil. Don't use too much or the excess will drip on the points and cause them to burn prematurely.

Table 2　　IGNITION ADVANCE

Models	Strokes	From Engine Number	To Engine Number	Advance with Engine still	Extent of Autom. Advance	Total Advance with Engine running at 3,000 rpm	Flywheel Position 0°
160 Monza Junior	4	—	—	21°-23°	18°	39°-41°	32°-36°
250 GT	4	—	—	5°-8°	28°	33°-36°	0°
250 Monza	4	—	85.486	5°-8°	28°	33°-36°	6°-8°
	4	85.487	—	5°-8°	28°	33°-36°	0°
250 Mach 1	4	—	—	5°-8°	28°	33°-36°	0°
250 Mark 3, 1963-64	4	—	87.921	38°-41°	—	38°-41°	0°
	4	87.922	88.295	38°-41°	—	38°-41°	19°-21°
	4	88.296	—	38°-41°	—	38°-41°	32°-36°
250 Mark 3, 1965-66	4	—	—	21°-23°	18°	39°-41°	32°-36°
250 Motocross	4	—	87.421	38°-41°	—	38°-41°	0°
	4	87.422	87.902	38°-41°	—	38°-41°	19°-21°
	4	87.903	—	21°-23°	18°	39°-41°	32°-36°
	4	—	—	5°-8°	28°	28°	0°
350 Sebring	4	—	—	5°-8°	28°	33°-36°	0°
450 Mk. 3, Desmo, Scr.	4	—	—	0°	28°	28°	0°
450 Desmo, cross, special	4	—	—	7°	18°	25°-30°	0°

Ignition Timing, Strobe Light

Setting the points on an electronic or magneto system requires the use of a strobe light. The best units have a separate power source for the light and are bright enough to use in daylight.

1. Remove the plug on the left side of the engine case and mount the indicator as shown in **Figure 16**.

2. Connect the strobe lead between the coil and spark plug.

3. Start the engine and let it run at 2,500 or 3,000 rpm. Aim the strobe at the indicator on the case side. The light should freeze the motion of the indicator when it is aligned with the timing mark as shown in **Figure 17**.

4. If the timing is incorrect, follow the procedures outlined previously for electronic or conventional ignition systems.

Headlight Adjustment

Proper headlight adjustment is essential to safe night riding. If the lights are set too low, the road will be invisible. If set too high, they will blind oncoming cars. Adjustment is very simple and should be a part of routine maintenance. The procedure is as follows.

1. Place the machine approximately 16 feet from a white or light colored wall. Refer to **Figure 18**.

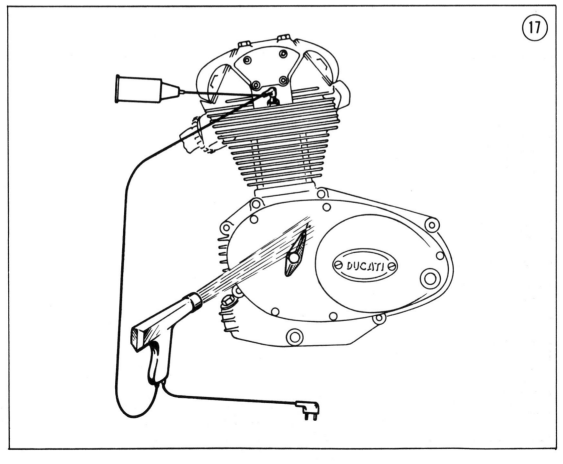

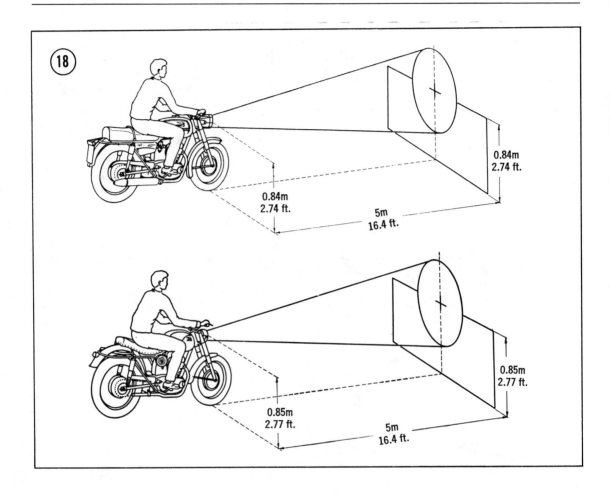

2. Make sure the bike and wall are on level, parallel ground and that the machine is pointing directly ahead.

3. Measurements should be made with one rider sitting on the bike and both wheels on the ground.

4. Draw a cross on the wall equal in height to the center of the headlight. This should be approximately 33 inches depending on the model.

5. Put on the high beam. The cross should be centered in the concentrated beam of light.

6. If the light does not correspond to the mark, loosen the two bolts and adjust. Tighten the bolts and recheck positioning.

WIRING DIAGRAM
(160 Monza Jr.)

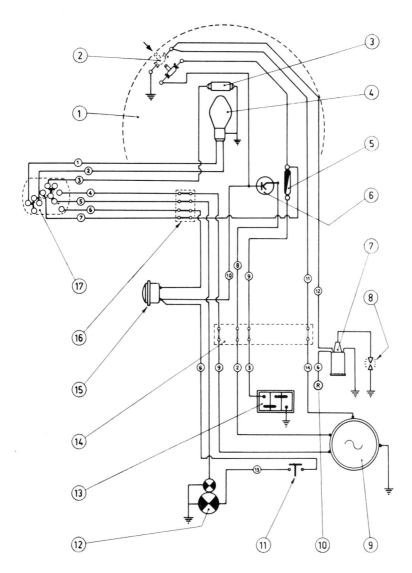

1. Headlight
2. Ignition switch
3. Parking light, 6V-3W
4. Headlight bulb, 6V-25/25W
5. Fuse, 15A
6. Diode
7. AC coil, 6V
8. Spark plug
9. Generator, 6V-28W
10. Contact breaker - condenser
11. Stop switch

12. License plate and stoplight bulbs, 6V-3/15W
13. Battery, 7Ah, 6V
14. Frame terminal block
15. Horn, 6V
16. Derivation terminal block
17. Light switch

COLOR CODE

1 = White
2 = White
3 = Blue
4 = Brown
5 = Black with yellow stripe
6 = Black
7 = Green
8 = Blue
9 = Red
10 = Black with blue stripe
11 = Green
12 = Green
13 = Black
14 = Yellow

WIRING DIAGRAM
(250 Scrambler up to Engine No. 92171 and Mark 3)

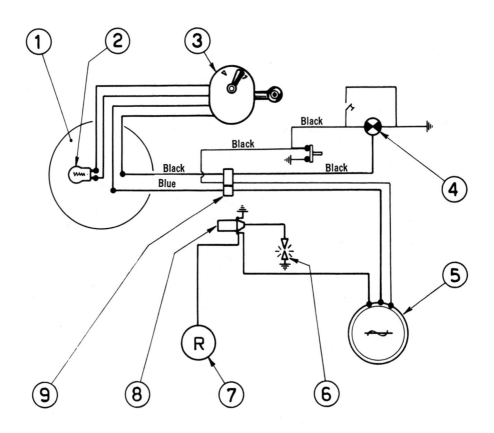

1. Headlight
2. 2-filament bulb, 6V-25/25W
3. Switch
4. Taillight, 6V-5/20W
5. Flywheel alternator, 6V-40W
6. Spark plug
7. Contact breaker-condenser
8. Alternator current ignition coil, 6V
9. 3-way terminal block

WIRING DIAGRAM
(250 Scrambler from Engine No. 92172)

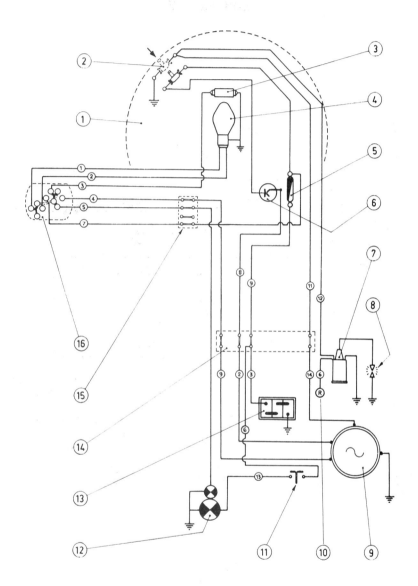

3

1. Headlight
2. Ignition key switch
3. Parking light, 6V-3W
4. Headlight bulb, 6V-25/25W
5. Fuse, 15A
6. Diode
7. AC coil, 6V
8. Spark plug
9. Generator, 6V-28W
10. Contact breaker - condenser
11. Stoplight switch

12. License plate and stoplight bulbs, 6V-3/15W
13. Battery, 7Ah-6V
14. Frame terminal block
15. Derivation terminal block
16. Light control switch

COLOR CODE
1 = White
2 = White
3 = Blue

4 = Brown
5 = Black with yellow stripe
6 = Black
7 = Green
8 = Blue
9 = Red
10 = Black with blue stripe
11 = Green
12 = Green
13 = Black
14 = Yellow

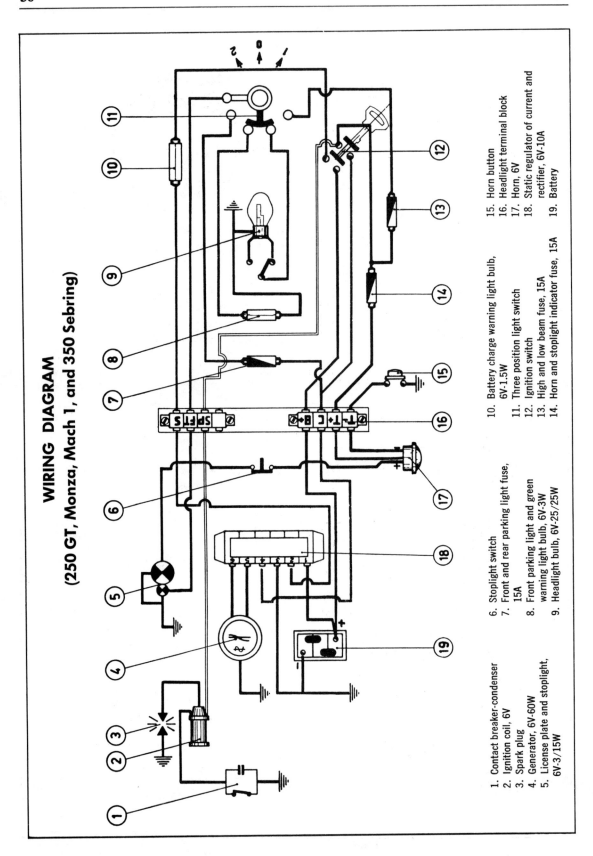

WIRING DIAGRAM
(250 GT, Monza, Mach 1, and 350 Sebring)

1. Contact breaker-condenser
2. Ignition coil, 6V
3. Spark plug
4. Generator, 6V-60W
5. License plate and stoplight, 6V-3/15W
6. Stoplight switch
7. Front and rear parking light fuse, 15A
8. Front parking light and green warning light bulb, 6V-3W
9. Headlight bulb, 6V-25/25W
10. Battery charge warning light bulb, 6V-1.5W
11. Three position light switch
12. Ignition switch
13. High and low beam fuse, 15A
14. Horn and stoplight indicator fuse, 15A
15. Horn button
16. Headlight terminal block
17. Horn, 6V
18. Static regulator of current and rectifier, 6V-10A
19. Battery

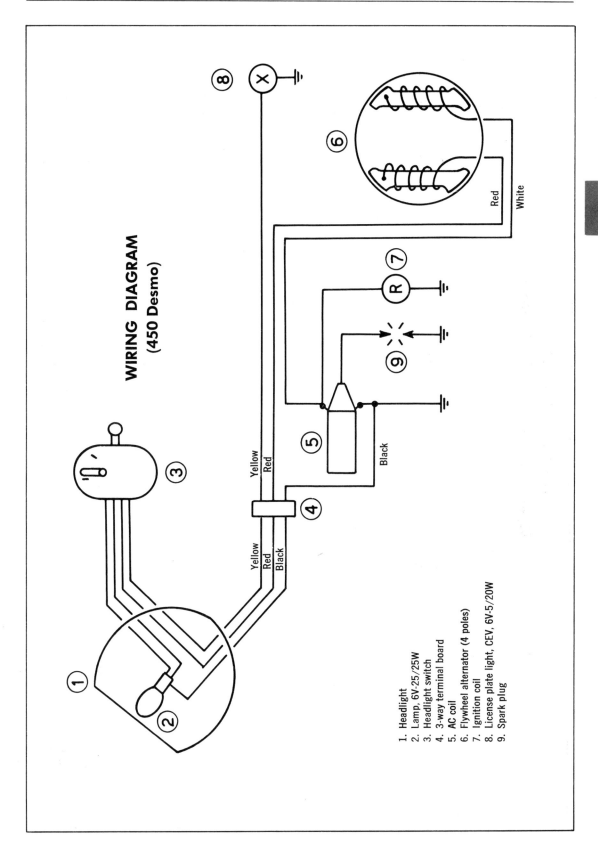

WIRING DIAGRAM
(450 Desmo)

1. Headlight
2. Lamp, 6V-25/25W
3. Headlight switch
4. 3-way terminal board
5. AC coil
6. Flywheel alternator (4 poles)
7. Ignition coil
8. License plate light, CEV, 6V-5/20W
9. Spark plug

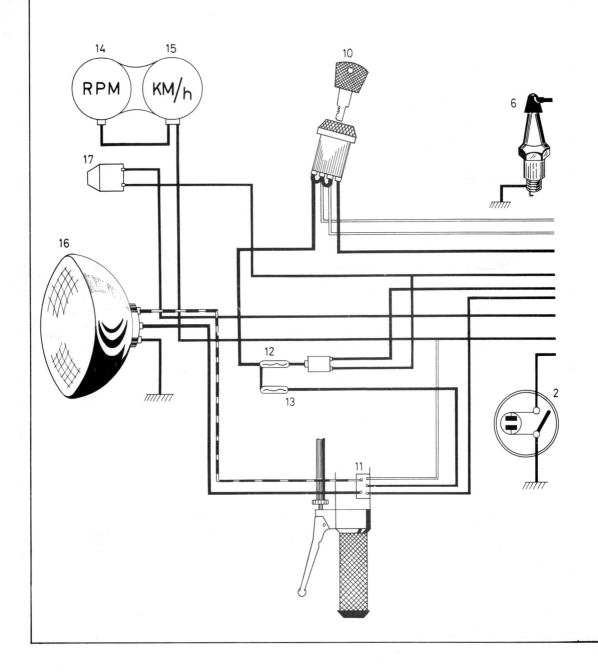

WIRING DIAGRAM — MODEL 250cc

1. Flywheel
2. Contact breaker - condenser
3. Electronic regulator
4. Battery
5. Ignition coil
6. Spark plug
7. Stoplight
8. Stoplight rear switch
9. Horn
10. Contact key
11. Light switch
12. Fuse
13. Fuse
14. Tachometer
15. Speedometer
16. Headlight
17. Stoplight front switch

3

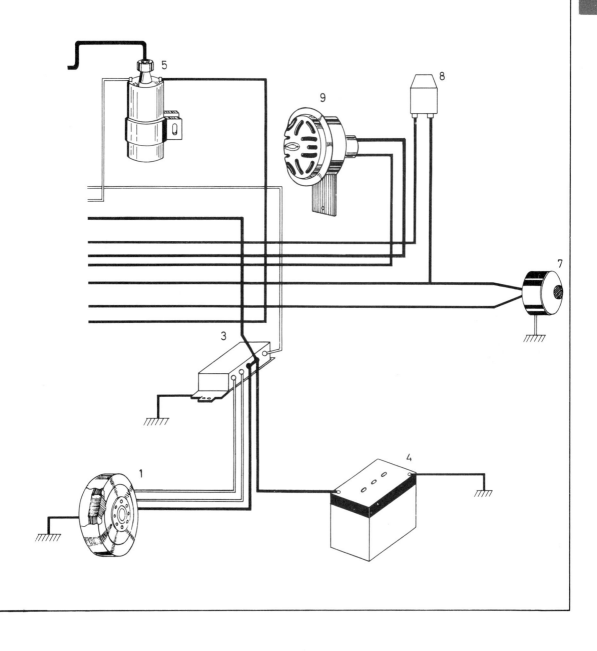

WIRING DIAGRAM — MODEL 350cc

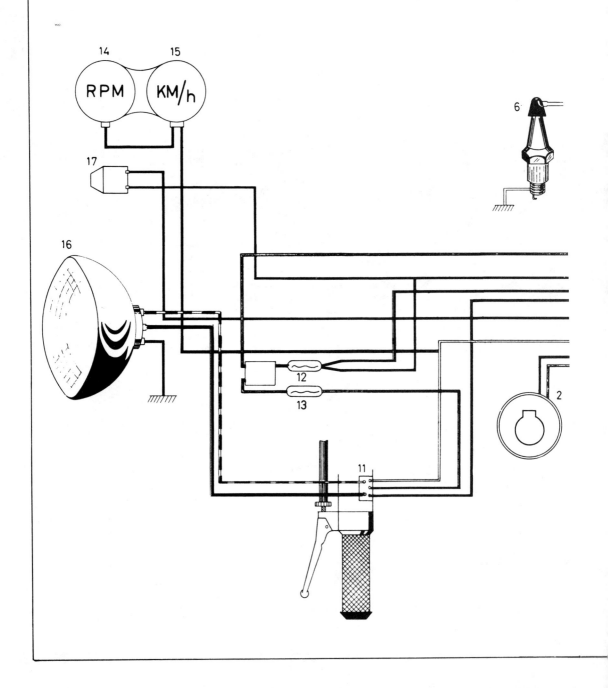

1. Flywheel
2. Pick-up
3. Electronic regulator
4. Battery
5. Electronic conversor
6. Spark plug
7. Stoplight
8. Stoplight rear switch
9. Horn

10. Contact key
11. Light switch
12. Fuse
13. Fuse
14. Tachometer
15. Speedometer
16. Headlight
17. Stoplight front switch

3

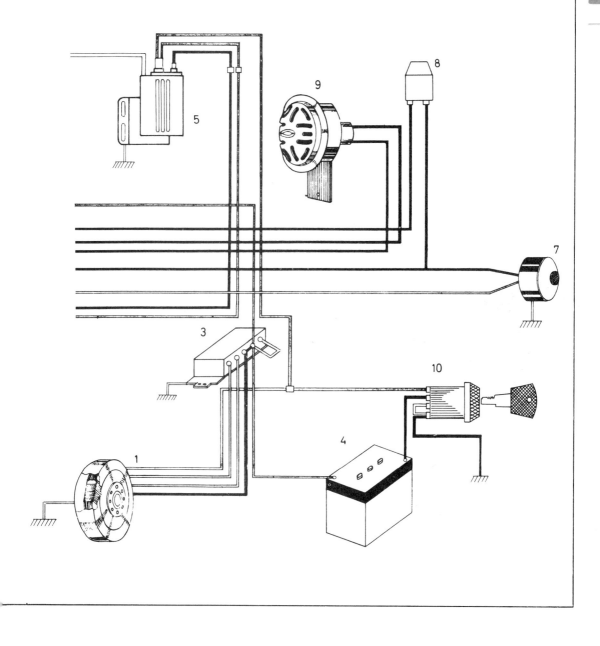

WIRING DIAGRAM
(450 Models: Mark 3, Mark 3 Desmo, SCR)

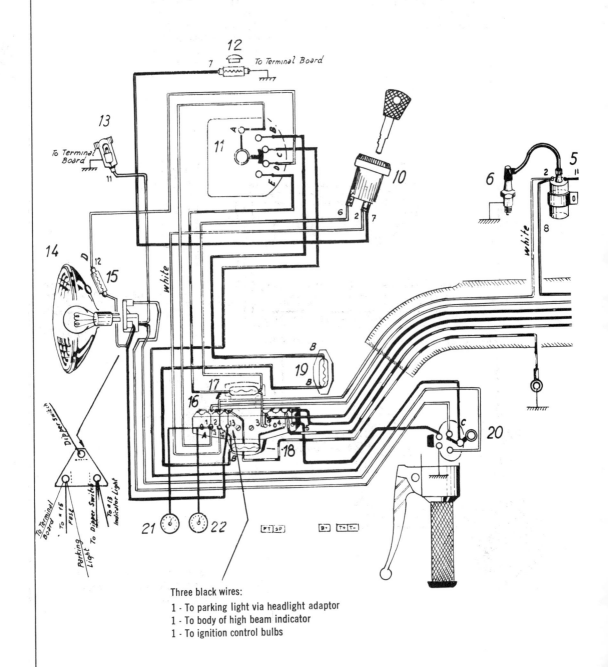

Three black wires:

1 - To parking light via headlight adaptor
1 - To body of high beam indicator
1 - To ignition control bulbs

1. Generator
2. Contact breaker - condenser
3. Electronic regulator
4. Battery
5. Ignition coil
6. Ignition spark plug
7. License plate and stoplight,
   6V - 3/15W
8. Stoplight switch
9. Horn
10. Ignition switch
11. Light switch
12. Ignition key control bulb, 6V - 1.5W

13. High beam red indicator
    lamp, 6V - 0.6W
14. Headlight bulb, 6V 25/25W
15. Parking light control
    green warning light, 6V - 3W
16. Headlight terminal board
17. Parking light fuse, 25 amp
18. Horn - stop fuse, 25 amp
19. High-low beam fuse, 25 amp
20. Dimmer and horn switch
21. Speedometer bulb, 12V - 3W
22. Tachometer bulb, 12V - 3W

3

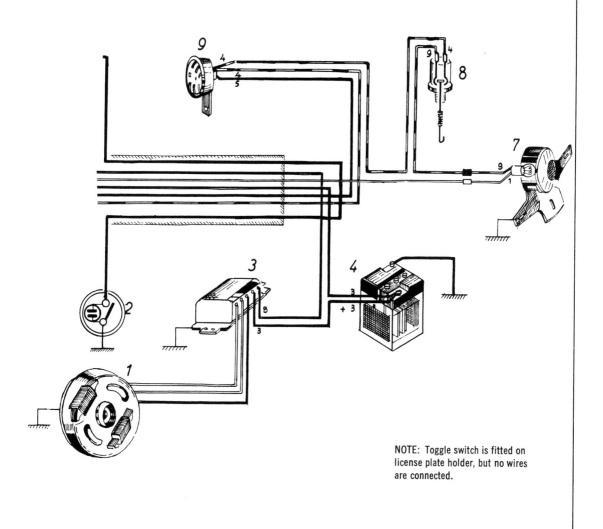

NOTE: Toggle switch is fitted on
license plate holder, but no wires
are connected.

CHAPTER FOUR

ENGINE

This chapter deals with procedures for removal, disassembly, replacement, reassembly, and installation of all Ducati single cylinder motorcycle engines. The procedures are specifically for the 250 GT but apply to all models. Much of the work can be performed on the engine while it is still in the frame. First, check the section which applies, then read it carefully to determine the extent of work required.

Illustrations are included to show differences between the engines and to simplify work. The illustrations are keyed to the text and to the type of bike. Study them carefully to avoid confusion. **Figure 1** is an exploded view of a typical Ducati engine.

ENGINE REMOVAL

The engine area should be carefully cleaned with a suitable solvent to simplify work. Kerosene or a commercial product, such as Gunk, can be used. Be careful not to use too heavy a concentration on painted surfaces. Rinse and wipe dry or blow off with compressed air.

1. Place a container or basin under the left side of the engine. Drain the oil by removing the drain plug and filter.

2. Turn off the fuel petcocks and disconnect the hoses.

3. Place a cloth next to the top of the forks, to protect the paint, and remove the tank.

4. Remove the seat and battery (if so equipped). Now would be an excellent time to top up the battery with distilled water and charge it according to the instructions in Chapter Three.

5. Disconnect the two yellow wires leading to the ignition system and wrap together to keep them out of the way. Disconnect all wires that may interfere with engine removal later. The wires are color coded for easy assembly and shouldn't require marking.

6. Loosen the ring clamp screw on the carburetor and disconnect the flexible hose between the throat and air cleaner. Slide the carburetor aside but leave all cable intact until later.

7. Turn the rear wheel until the master connecting link is accessible. Remove the clip and chain. Replace the master link so that it will not be lost. Place the chain in a container large enough to allow oil to cover every link and allow it to soak in standard 30-weight oil for a few days. Several hours prior to reassembly, hang the chain by one end and allow excess oil to drip off. Remove the chain guard.

8. Loosen the screw which attaches the muffler to the frame. Swing the muffler out and loosen the retaining ring at the engine juncture. Lay the muffler aside carefully and wrap in cloth to protect the chrome finish.

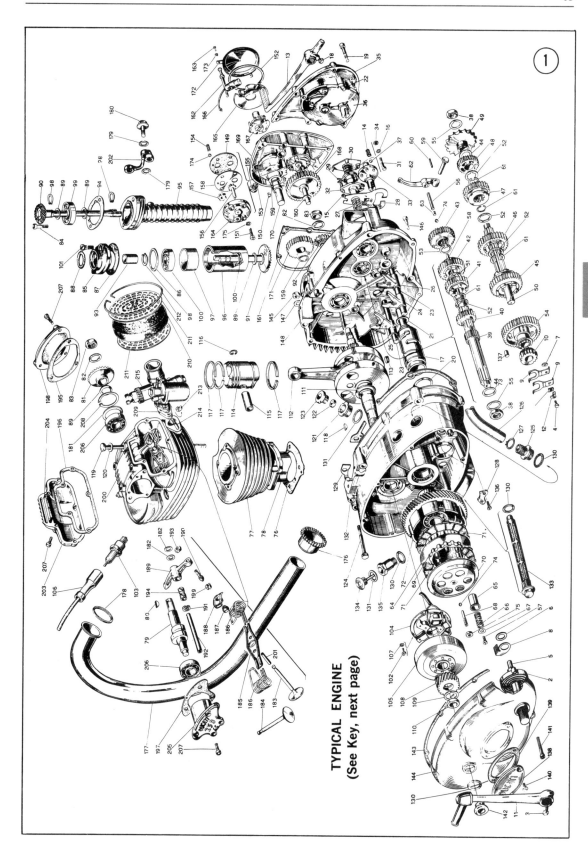

TYPICAL ENGINE
(See Key, next page)

①

TYPICAL DUCATI ENGINE

STARTER ASSEMBLY

1. Plate
2. Pedal return spring
3. Screw
4. Screw
5. Starter pin
6. Thrust washer
7. Washer
8. Segment locking plate
9. Leaf spring
10. Starter gear
11. Complete starter lever
12. Safety washer

GEARBOX CONTROL ASSEMBLY

13. Gear operating lever
14. Ball spring
15. Washer
16. Bent washer
17. Speed gear selector
18. Screw
19. Screw
20. Thrust washer
21. Thrust washer
22. Screw
23. Fork pin
24. 1st and 3rd speed engaging fork
25. 2nd and 4th speed engaging fork
26. Top speed engaging fork
27. Fork pressure spring
28. Selector operating fork
29. Pedal return spring
30. Adjustment plate
31. Eccentric
32. Fork operating spindle
33. 5th speed selector
34. Hexagon nut
35. Cover, chain side
36. Cover for speed selector
37. 11/32" ball

GEARSHIFT & CLUTCH ASSEMBLY

38. Hexagon nut
39. Gear change main shaft
40. 2nd speed driving gear
41. 3rd speed driving gear
42. 4th speed driving gear
43. 5th speed driving gear
44. Washer
45. 2nd speed driven gear
46. 3rd speed driven gear
47. 4th speed driven gear
48. 5th speed driven gear
49. Chain sprocket
50. Gearbox layshaft
51. Grooved thrust washer
52. Grooved thrust washer
53. Spring ring
54. 1st speed driven gear
55. Safety washer tab
56. Clutch peg
57. Screw
58. Clutch operating rod
59. Clutch lever pin
60. Split drift pin
61. Spring ring
62. Clutch operating lever
63. Roller
64. Inner driven disc
65. Spring retainer
66. Clutch spring
67. Washer
68. Clutch adjustment screw
69. Clutch drum
70. Pressure disc
71. Driving disc
72. Clutch housing
73. Outer spacer
74. Ball 3/16"
75. Hexagon nut

CYLINDER ASSEMBLY

76. Cylinder-to-head gasket
77. Cylinder
78. Cylinder liner

TIMING ASSEMBLY

79. Timing shaft
80. Special Woodruff key
81. Bevel gear
82. Safety washer with tab
83. Hexagon nut
84. Screw
85. Flange
86. Thrust washer
87. Flange-to-crankcase gasket
88. Gasket
89. Normal thrust washer
90. Transmission with bevel gear
91. Bevel gear
92. Bevel gear
93. Normal sleeve
94. Gasket for head protection
95. Timing protection
96. Bushing
97. Spacer
98. Circlip
99. Bearing
100. Bearing
101. Screw

ELECTRIC SYSTEM ASSEMBLY

102. Screw
103. Spark plug with gasket
104. Complete stator plate
105. Flywheel
106. Ignition cable
107. Spring washer

CRANKSHAFT ASSEMBLY

108. Crankshaft gear
109. Safety washer with tab
110. Hexagon nut
111. Thrust washer
112. Crankshaft
113. Threaded dowel
114. Complete normal Borgo piston
115. Normal piston pin
116. Spring ring
117. Piston rings set
118. Woodruff key

CRANKCASE ASSEMBLY

119. Tie rod
120. Bent washer
121. Cable gland nut
122. Rubber for flywheel cable
123. Ring plug
124. Screw
125. Breather air nozzle
126. Breather tube
127. Breather tube locking ring
128. Plate
129. Gasket
130. Gasket
131. Gasket
132. Crankcase, clutch side
133. Filter
134. Oil plug with dipstick

135. Oil filler
136. Screw
137. Roller
138. Clutch adjustment hole cover
139. Cover gasket
140. Screw
141. Screw
142. Plug
143. Clutch side cover gasket
144. Clutch side cover with bushing
145. Hexagon nut
146. Screw
147. Bent washer
148. Crankcase, chain side

PUMP - ELECTRICAL SYSTEM ASSEMBLY

149. Pump gasket
150. Special Woodruff key
151. Screw with hole
152. Gasket
153. Rubber tube
154. Pressure valve spring
155. Threaded bushing
156. Driving gear
157. Driven gear
158. Pump cover
159. Thrust washer
160. Thrust washer
161. Timing cover gasket
162. Column
163. Screw

164. Pump body
165. Complete distributor
166. Condenser
167. Automatic advance
168. Pump operating gear with pin
169. Timing cover
170. Distributor operating spindle
171. Distributor driving gear
172. Distributor cover with 2 springs
173. Spring washer
174. ¼" ball
175. Spring washer

EXHAUST ASSEMBLY

176. Hold ring
177. Exhaust pipe
178. Gasket

HEAD ASSEMBLY

179. Gasket
180. Union screw
181. Thrust washer
182. Thrust washer
183. Inlet valve
184. Exhaust valve
185. Spring attachment cross-bar
186. Valve spring
187. Valve rubber
188. Tie spring attachment

189. Rocker with chromed shoe
190. Adjustment screw
191. Spring washer
192. Rocker pin
193. Hexagon nut
194. Rocker normal bushing
195. Timing cover gasket
196. Valve cover gasket
197. Cap gasket
198. Timing cover
199. Cotter pins
200. Head
201. Split spring drift
202. Oil union
203. Valve cover
204. Rubber
205. Cap bearing holder
206. Bearing
207. Screw
208. Circlip

CARBURETOR

209. Rubber spacer
210. Filtering body
211. Drilled disc
212. Filtering body retaining ring
213. Hexagon nut Elastic-Stop
214. Stud
215. Dell'Orto (type UBF 24 BS) carburetor

4

9. Remove the clamping ring and breather tube from the engine with a pair of pliers. Parts are easier to locate and match up later if kept with their respective components when disassembled. For instance, replace the clamp on the breather tube and set aside. Frame mounting screws can be replaced in their holes after a component has been removed.

10. Using a T-wrench or ratchet, unscrew the six screws of the shifting mechanism assembly and remove it completely. Disconnect the clutch control cable and lay it across the frame tube.

11. Loosen the foot rest bolts and allow the pegs to rotate out of the way.

12. Disconnect the distributor cable from the ignition coil.

13. Starting at the top rear of the engine, remove all engine mounting nuts and bolts. Replace the top rear bolt with a smooth shaft, to allow the engine to move freely, prior to removing the remaining nuts and bolts. Support the engine at the front to keep it from dropping out as bolts are removed. Support the engine at the front with your right hand and remove the pin at the rear. Swing the engine to the right and carefully slide it out of the frame being careful not to damage the ignition coil. A homemade engine work stand can be fabricated out of scrap lumber. Form a box of 2 x 4's, 12 inches by 18 inches, and set the engine on this. The engine can now be maneuvered for convenience.

Engine Dismantling

1. Loosen the four cylinder head screws a quarter of a turn each until loose enough to remove by hand. Complete removal of each screw in turn could cause undue pressure and warping of the head.

2. Loosen the two screws securing the timing gear cover to the crankcase and lift off. See **Figure 2**.

3. Twist the cylinder head slightly and lift off. Corrosion may have caused the head to bind to the cylinder; tap the edges of the intake and exhaust flanges lightly with a rubber or leather mallet while applying pressure to the head. Never tap on the fin surfaces as they are easily damaged and broken.

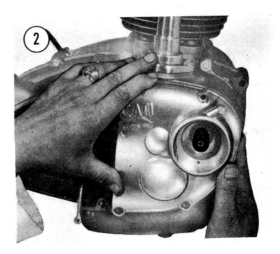

4. Check the condition of the head gasket to determine if it can be reused. If in doubt, replace.

5. Rock the cylinder and pull it slightly away from the cases. Place a clean shop rag in the opening under the piston to prevent debris from entering the cases. Continue to rock and remove the cylinder.

6. Support the piston and remove the wrist pin clip with a pair of needle nose pliers. During assembly, use a new clip or a Teflon button. This one inexpensive item is extremely critical to engine longevity. A used clip could allow the wrist pin to shift and score the cylinder wall while running.

7. Support the piston and tap out the wrist pin. A small socket and extension can be used as a tool for this purpose. Be careful to prevent any damage to the connecting rod. A bent rod can impair performance or cause severe damage. This is as far as the engine needs to be dismantled for repairs to the piston or top end. Fortunately, most damage and periodic repair excludes the transmission. The clutch is accessible without splitting the cases.

Dismantling the Cylinder Head

1. Remove the camshaft covers by loosening the three screws on each unit.

2. Remove the four screws retaining the bearing carrier and cover plate. Insert a pin or rod from the opposite side and gently tap out the cap.

3. Remove the camshaft carrier cover and its gasket.

4. The rocker shafts must be removed using the special extractor.

5. Remove the springs and spacing washers.

Camshaft and Gear Removal

1. Straighten the tabs on the washer.

2. Insert special tool Number 15 from the cap end to hold the camshaft in position, as shown in **Figure 3**.

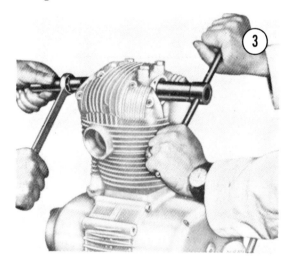

3. Use a 22mm wrench to hold the nut and loosen the camshaft screw. See **Figure 4**.

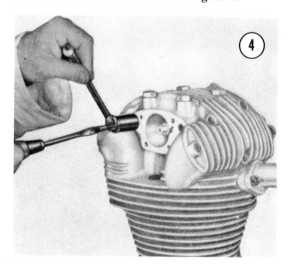

4. Remove the special tool and drive the camshaft out of the cap side.

5. Remove the gear, Woodruff key, and spacing washers.

Removing the Valves

1. Use a valve spring compressor to apply pressure to the valve springs and remove the half-cones and spring saddles at the end of the valve stem. See **Figure 5**.

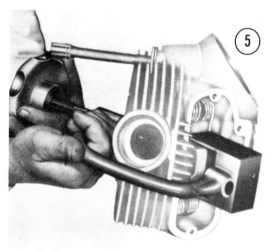

2. Release the compressor and slip the valves out of their guides. Keep each valve and attendant pieces separate as the parts are not interchangeable.

Camshaft Drive Cover Removal

1. Use a 17mm wrench to remove the oil return lines.

2. Pull the cover out along with the driver, bearing, and bearing carrier.

3. Dislodge the circlips, keeping the shims on either side of the bearing separate.

4. Note the location of each of the shims for reassembly since they appear to be identical.

Clutch Removal

1. Remove the right side crankcase cover and secure the main shaft gear.

2. Straighten the tabs of the locking washer and loosen the timing gear shaft nut. This particular nut has left-hand threads and must be turned counterclockwise as shown in **Figure 6**. Tie the gear and washers together with string to store until reassembly.

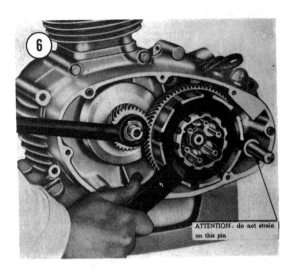

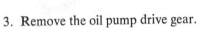

3. Remove the oil pump drive gear.

4. Hold the countershaft sprocket in place with the special tool and remove the nut as shown in **Figure 7**.

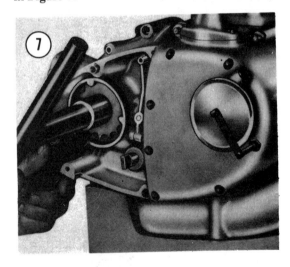

5. Slide the gear off its shaft.

6. Unbolt the kickstarter lever and remove.

7. Remove the crankcase cover screws with an Allen wrench.

8. Insert the puller in the threaded hole in the center of the case cover, **Figure 8**.

9. Maintain pressure with the extractor and lightly tap the edges of the case with a rubber mallet to remove. Never use a screwdriver or other sharp instrument on the cover or the gasket mating surfaces will be damaged.

10. The shim washer may stick to the cover and

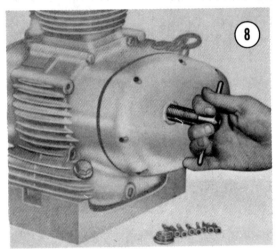

should be removed. Remove the clutch springs and screws.

11. Use a screwdriver to remove the clutch spring cups.

12. Remove the clutch pressure plate and discs.

13. Open the tabs on the locking washer with a screwdriver.

14. Hold the clutch housing in place with the special tool as shown in **Figure 9**. A similar tool can be made from an old steel clutch plate and bar stock welded together. Another method for securing the housing is to wedge a shop rag between the gears on the bottom running edge as pressure is applied to the hub nut.

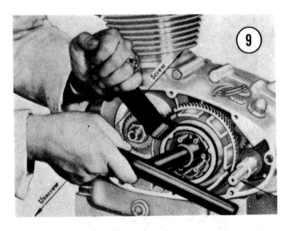

15. Remove the clutch hub with the special puller as shown in **Figure 10**. This tool is similar to a universal gear puller which is easy to obtain and can be used for other jobs.

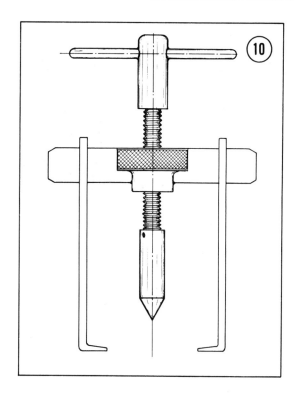

16. Bend the tabs on the locking washer and remove the screw and leaf springs.

17. Pull the starter gear out.

Magneto Removal

The flywheel is always a snug fit on its shaft and must be extracted using a special tool as shown in **Figure 11**.

Stator Removal

1. Remove the bakelite cable plug.

2. Use an open end wrench and remove the cable nut.

3. Loosen the screws that secure the stator. When storing the stator and flywheel magneto, place them so the windings are protected and away from any magnetic material.

4. Insert a 4mm diameter rod into the main shaft hole and push out the clutch pushrod, control spindle, roller, and two balls.

Splitting the Cases

1. Remove the two 8mm bolts with a 14mm wrench.

2. Remove the five Allen head screws. The cases are now ready to come apart.

3. Place the engine upright and lightly tap on the end of the main shaft. Check frequently to see if the cases are separating cleanly.

4. Turn the engine over, so that the chain side rests on the bench, as soon as the cases are free of the locating bushings. The remaining clutch half can be lifted free.

5. The gear box and crank assemblies will be in the chain half of the two cases. On all four-speed models, the gear will have to be removed when the crankcase is lifted. A special plate is available from Ducati in the event that the cases are difficult to separate. See **Figure 12**.

6. Use an aluminum drift and tap out the first

gear from the hub side of the case.

7. Check the starting plate for signs of damage and the tightness of the retaining screws.

8. Remove the crank assembly by hand, tapping lightly with a mallet as it is drawn out. Note the location and order of the shim washers. Other parts removed at this stage include the gearshift forks, guide rods, cam drum, gear change main shaft, and layshaft.

9. Use a pair of needle nose pliers to remove the circlip from bevel gear Z-30.

10. Tap on the stem of gear Z-30 with an aluminum drift until it drops free.

11. Extract the bushings and related bearings.

Crankcase Bearing and Bushing Removal

This operation needs to be performed only if the replacement of bearings and bushings is really necessary. Check the bearings by rotating and listening for harsh sounds. Also check for side-play in the races. The bushings will need replacement if scored or burned.

1. Wash the two halves of the cases with kerosene and allow to dry thoroughly.

2. Heat the two halves on an electric hot plate until they reach a temperature of 180-210° F.

3. Tap the bearings out using an aluminum drift. Take care not to allow the bearings to shift or the housing may warp. The same method is used to remove the bushings and shell. Never heat them over an open flame or with a torch.

4. Have the appropriate gears and bushings ready for reinstallation at this time. Heating the cases more than once increases the chance for warpage. When inserting the new bearings, be sure the lettering on the race faces outward.

5. When the cases have had time to cool, check the bearings for tightness and location. The bearings and bushings can also be removed and installed on a partially assembled, cold engine using the special bearing extractors shown in **Figures 13, 14, 15, and 16**.

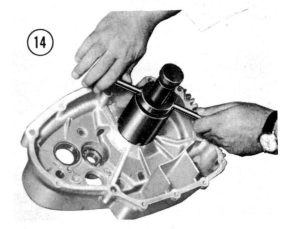

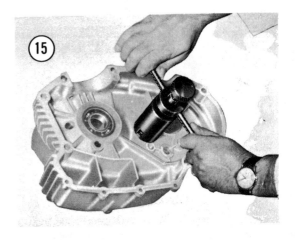

Dismantling the Timing Cover

1. Use a screwdriver to remove the screw and automatic advance.

2. Remove the two screws and the ignition plate. Place these parts in a box.

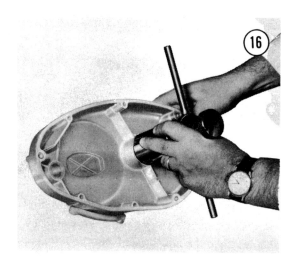

3. To dismantle the pump, break the lead seals, loosen the four screws and free the body by hand. The two inside gears, pump cover, gasket, ball, and spring will also be freed.

Removing Cylinder Liner

This procedure sounds more complicated than it actually is. A press could be used on a cold cylinder, but the average mechanic will find it easier to follow these steps.

1. Place the new liner in a refrigerator prior to starting on this job.

2. Heat the cylinder on a hot plate until it stabilizes at 180-210° F.

3. Lift the cylinder and allow the liner to drop out. A cold rag inserted in the liner may allow more clearance.

4. Insert the new liner immediately before the cylinder has had time to cool. Line up the four cutaways carefully before the cylinder cools and hold in place until trapped by the shrinking metal.

5. Check the top and bottom surfaces for match and make sure the oil hole is clean.

ENGINE ASSEMBLY

While the engine is completely disassembled, check all components which may be subject to wear or damage and repair or replace as needed. The additional cost of some items is small compared to the amount of work and money re-

quired for later repair caused by negligence or penny-pinching at this stage.

Adjusting tolerances of some components requires the simple addition of inexpensive shim washers which are available in a variety of sizes.

Not all damage or wear is obvious to the naked eye. Special measuring instruments, such as feeler gauges, micrometers or calipers, are needed to determine the amount of wear and limits of acceptability. Several tables are included on the popular models to indicate limits of wear. Consult these tables, in Chapter Two, as assembly progresses.

The procedures outlined in the disassembly section can be reversed and used as a general guide for reassembly. Specific operations and limits are outlined in detail in this section.

The exploded view of the engine components, Figure 1, is the best possible aid to accurate placement of parts within the engine. The accompanying parts list gives the size and description of each part and shows the relative position in relation to other parts. Refer to this illustration frequently as work progresses. The illustration can also be used as an aid in ordering needed parts.

Bearing Housing Installation

1. Thread the Z-30 bevel gear from the bottom of the crankcase into the housing which has been inserted from the top. See **Figure 17**.

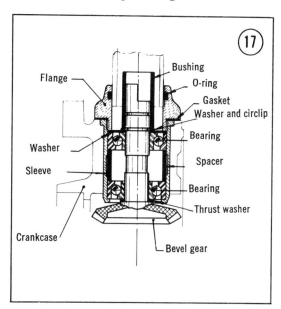

2. Install another thrust washer and hold in place with a circlip.

3. Check for excessive end-play and correct with larger shims.

4. Place the thrust washer on top of the bearing and assemble with the flange gasket.

5. Install the flange and related O-ring.

6. Use a feeler gauge to determine if the gasket is well seated and shim, if necessary, with thinner washers.

7. Install the coupling sleeve over the gear shaft.

Crankshaft Installation

1. Place the chain side of the crankcase on the engine box as shown in **Figure 18**.

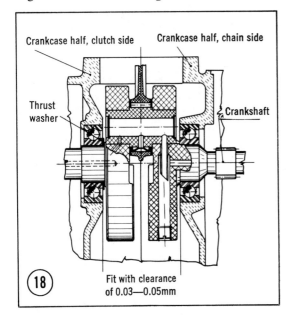

Crankcase half, clutch side   Crankcase half, chain side

Thrust washer

Crankshaft

18

Fit with clearance of 0.03—0.05mm

2. Insert the driving gear end of the crankshaft in its bearing and seat by tapping with a mallet. If the fit is too tight, polish the outer diameter of the shaft with emery cloth. Make sure the shaft is seated against the bearing.

3. Install shim washers on free end of shaft.

4. Install the clutch side of the case and test the shaft for smoothness of operation. End-play must not exceed the limits of .0012-.0020 in. (0.03-0.05mm). Replace the shims as needed to bring within specifications. It's best to start with a tight fit adjusting gradually until the shaft is just free to move.

Gearbox Assembly

1. Put the first speed gear (kickstarter gear) in the left case with the rollers. Use grease to hold the pieces together and to provide lubrication. See **Figure 19**.

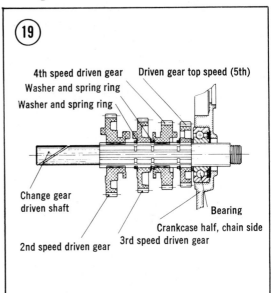

19

4th speed driven gear   Driven gear top speed (5th)
Washer and spring ring
Washer and spring ring

Change gear driven shaft

Bearing

Crankcase half, chain side

2nd speed driven gear   3rd speed driven gear

2. Test the gears on the layshaft to make sure they slide freely and have proper teeth mesh.

3. Slide the layshaft, complete with gears, into its bearing and tap lightly into place. See **Figure 20**.

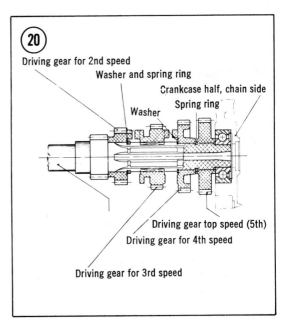

20

Driving gear for 2nd speed
Washer and spring ring
Crankcase half, chain side
Spring ring
Washer

Driving gear top speed (5th)
Driving gear for 4th speed

Driving gear for 3rd speed

4. Insert the cam drum and two shim washers. Be sure the drum rotates freely.

5. Insert the three shifting forks between the appropriate gears, then engage the opposite ends into the drum.

6. Insert the fork guides through the forks and into the crankcase bosses as shown in **Figure 21**. If any of the parts bind or fail to function properly, recheck assembly.

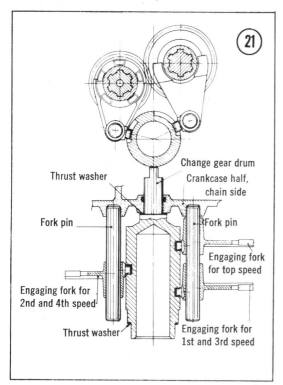

Thrust washer

Change gear drum

Crankcase half, chain side

Fork pin

Fork pin

Engaging fork for top speed

Engaging fork for 2nd and 4th speed

Thrust washer

Engaging fork for 1st and 3rd speed

Crankcase Reassembly

1. Place a new gasket in position on one of the case surfaces being careful to leave the oil passage exposed.

2. Fit the two cases together.

3. Rotate the gearbox shaft while tapping on the case edges to allow the two to settle in place.

4. Put the proper screws in place and tighten until snug. Tighten the screws where opposite sides are taken in sequence. Never tighten screws adjacent to one another to prevent warpage of the gasket mating surfaces.

5. Tap around the inner race of the crankshaft bearing to release any pressure which may have accumulated during assembly.

Oil Filter Assembly

1. Place the washer on the threaded end of the oil filter and thread it into the clutch side of the cases as shown in **Figure 22**.

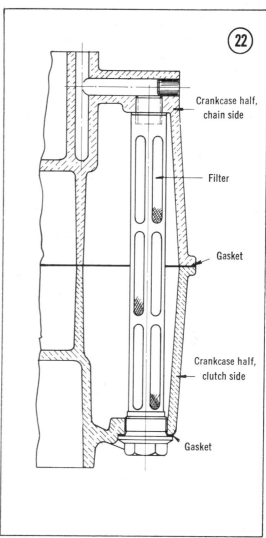

Crankcase half, chain side

Filter

Gasket

Crankcase half, clutch side

Gasket

2. Install the pump gear and its washer.

3. Slide the shim washer on the driving shaft. Insert the Woodruff key and bevel gear so the timing marks on the two mating gears coincide as shown in **Figure 23**.

4. Rotate the gears by hand until the ground surfaces are in view and flush with one another. At this point, the gears should be perfectly meshed and should rotate without backlash. Shim if necessary until the above described conditions are met.

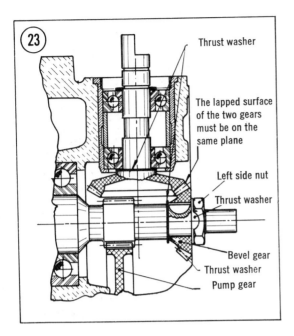

The lapped surface of the two gears must be on the same plane

Thrust washer

Left side nut

Thrust washer

Bevel gear

Thrust washer

Pump gear

Magneto Assembly

Install the stator, using the screws and washers, on the left side of the cases. Refer to the *Magneto* section of Chapter Three for timing and **Figure 24** for details of installation.

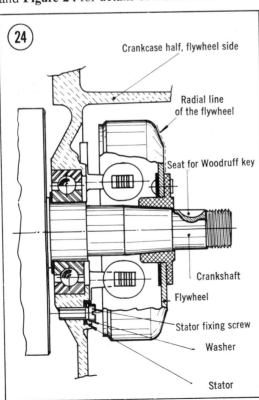

Crankcase half, flywheel side

Radial line of the flywheel

Seat for Woodruff key

Crankshaft

Flywheel

Stator fixing screw

Washer

Stator

Kickstarter Assembly

1. Fit the starter gear and spindle assembly, complete with spring, spacer, thrust washer, and lock plate, together as shown in **Figure 25**.

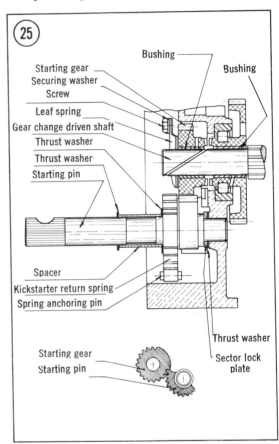

Bushing

Bushing

Starting gear
Securing washer
Screw
Leaf spring
Gear change driven shaft
Thrust washer
Thrust washer
Starting pin

Spacer
Kickstarter return spring
Spring anchoring pin

Thrust washer

Starting gear
Starting pin

Sector lock plate

2. Wind the spring until it can be attached to the anchor point. Install the leaf spring and secure with the plate and washer.

3. Check the position of the fingers to be sure they are equal distant from center of shaft.

4. Lock the bolt by lifting a tab of the lock-washer over its head and lowering the other tab against the case.

5. Fit the Woodruff key and driving gear to the crankshaft.

Clutch Assembly

1. Place the spacer on the clutch main shaft and position the bearing within its housing.

2. Slide the clutch drum and safety washer in place and secure with the nut. Hold the drum

firm (**Figure 26**) and tighten with a torque wrench to 700-850 ft-lbs. as shown in **Figure 27**.

3. Rotate the clutch drum to make sure it turns smoothly and there is no end-play. If the driving gear and clutch housing mesh too tightly, the engine will whine and a smaller driving gear

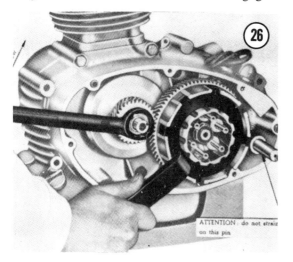

must be fitted. Excessive play will cause rattling.

4. Lock the nut by turning the tabs up on the locking washer.

5. Install the clutch plates starting with one cork covered disc and alternating with steel as shown in **Figure 28**.

6. Insert the clutch peg, ball, clutch actuating

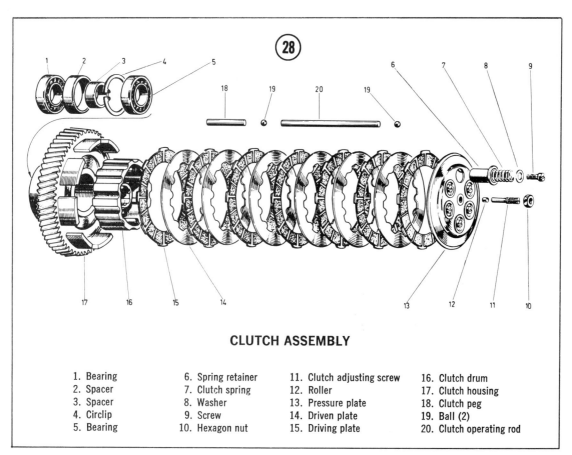

CLUTCH ASSEMBLY

1. Bearing	6. Spring retainer	11. Clutch adjusting screw	16. Clutch drum
2. Spacer	7. Clutch spring	12. Roller	17. Clutch housing
3. Spacer	8. Washer	13. Pressure plate	18. Clutch peg
4. Circlip	9. Screw	14. Driven plate	19. Ball (2)
5. Bearing	10. Hexagon nut	15. Driving plate	20. Clutch operating rod

rod, second ball, and roller into the mainshaft cavity. See **Figure 29** for details.

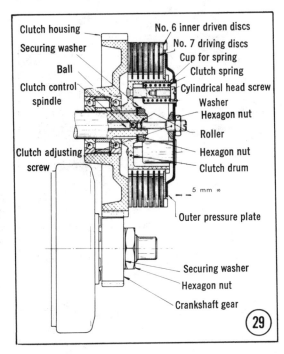

Clutch housing
No. 6 inner driven discs
Securing washer
No. 7 driving discs
Ball
Cup for spring
Clutch control spindle
Clutch spring
Cylindrical head screw
Washer
Hexagon nut
Roller
Clutch adjusting screw
Hexagon nut
Clutch drum
5 mm
Outer pressure plate
Securing washer
Hexagon nut
Crankshaft gear

29

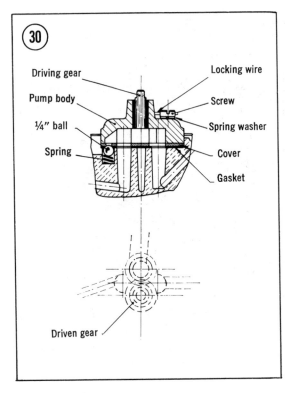

30

Driving gear
Locking wire
Pump body
Screw
¼" ball
Spring washer
Spring
Cover
Gasket
Driven gear

7. Install the pressure plate with adjustment screw and nut.

8. Insert the springs in the retaining cups and, in turn, into the pressure plate holes. Tighten all screws.

9. Adjust the pressure plate leaving the screw to protrude 0.2 inch (5mm) and tighten the nut.

10. Position a new cover gasket on the outer half-cover and install on the case.

11. Insert the oil seal rubber in the starter spindle.

12. Position the kickstarter lever so that it is declined 45° toward the rear of the engine and tighten the securing nut.

Pump Installation

1. Assemble the pump body, bushing, and pin. See **Figure 30**.

2. Insert the pressure valve spring and ball in the seat of the timing cover.

3. Insert the gears in the pump body and make sure they turn freely.

4. Check the clearance between the end faces of the gear and pump cover.

5. Coat the gears with heavy grease.

6. Assemble the gasket, cover, and body on the timing side cover.

7. Time the pump gear with the drive shaft gear by making sure the two marks coincide.

8. Time the advance gear (**Figure 31**) with the pump gear making sure the two marks coincide. Put the two thrust washers on the advance shaft.

9. Bolt in position and secure the cover while positioning with the special bushing as shown in **Figure 32**.

Automatic Advance and Distributor

1. Insert the automatic advance in the spindle with the cam lobe facing up and to the right.

2. Install the ignition distributor. Refer to Chapter Three for details on accurate timing.

Countershaft Sprocket

1. Assemble the sprocket, locking washer, and nut on the countershaft.

2. Hold sprocket in place and tighten nut.

3. Bend the ears of the washer over the head of the nut to secure.

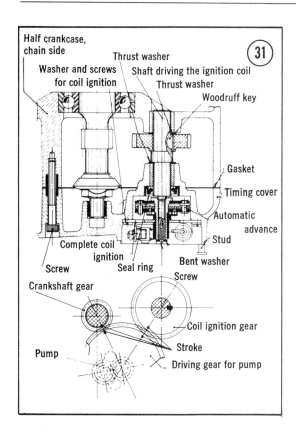

Figure 31: Half crankcase, chain side; Washer and screws for coil ignition; Thrust washer; Shaft driving the ignition coil; Thrust washer; Woodruff key; Gasket; Timing cover; Automatic advance; Stud; Bent washer; Screw; Coil ignition gear; Stroke; Driving gear for pump; Pump; Crankshaft gear; Screw; Seal ring; Complete coil ignition

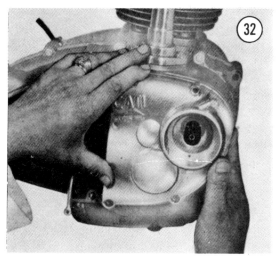

Figure 32

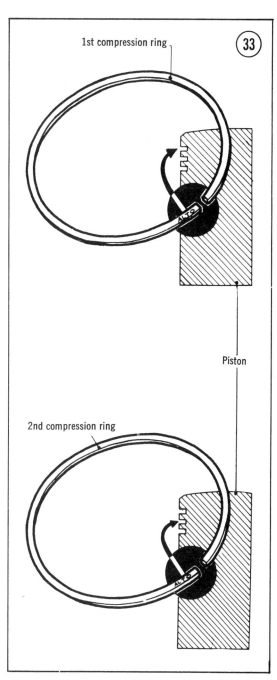

Figure 33: 1st compression ring; Piston; 2nd compression ring

Piston Assembly

1. If new rings are to be installed, make sure to place them on the piston with the word "Alto" facing up as shown in **Figure 33**.

2. Start from the top of the piston and slide the third (scraper ring) in place within its groove. Be careful not to bend or break any of the rings.

Place the remaining two compression rings in their respective slots.

3. Unlike most other bikes, the Ducati is fitted with a third scraper ring at the bottom of the piston.

4. Heat the piston to 140-180° F by placing in hot oil, or on a hot plate, or by heating the crown with a torch.

5. Place the piston in position over the connecting rod so that the smallest of the two crown dimples faces the front of the engine (**Figure 34**).

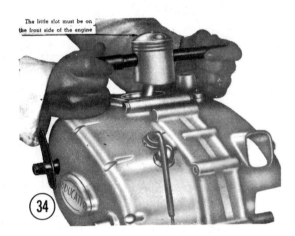

The little slot must be on the front side of the engine

6. Align the wrist pin hole with the rod and drive the pin in place with a drift. The piston should still be warm enough to allow the pin to slip in easily. If not, cool the pin in a refrigerator for 30 minutes and reheat the piston in oil. Never force the wrist pin without supporting the rod.

7. Retain the pin with 2 new clips or Teflon buttons.

Installing the Cylinder

1. First clean the gasket mating surfaces with kerosene.

2. Install a new base gasket. Some mechanics prefer to use a gasket sealing compound, such as Gascacinch, to ensure a perfect seal but this isn't necessary and only complicates subsequent teardown operations.

3. Stagger the piston ring gaps so that they are not in line with each other or with the connecting rod cutout in the barrel (**Figure 35**). If any two rings do align it could cause excessive blow-by.

4. Lubricate the piston and rings by smearing with 30-weight motor oil compatible with the oil to be used in the crankcase.

5. Make sure the small O-ring is fitted in place over the hollow oil lubricating stud.

6. Slide the cylinder in place and carefully fit

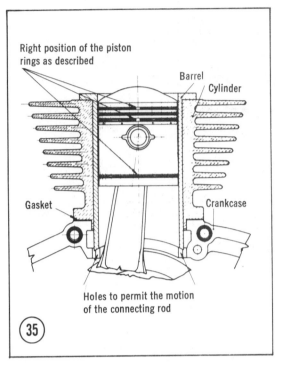

Right position of the piston rings as described

Barrel / Cylinder

Gasket   Crankcase

Holes to permit the motion of the connecting rod

each ring in the barrel. The base of the barrel is chamfered to simplify fitting but a special ring compressing tool may help.

Cylinder Head

1. Lapping the valves is a simple operation and should be performed while the engine is apart.

2. Coat the valve head and seating area with valve grinding compound or a mixture of oil and a fine abrasive.

3. Insert the valve in its seat and grip the end of the stem. A special tool (**Figure 36**) is made for this purpose but most automotive supply stores carry a universal type which can be used on other engines.

4. Pull on the stem and rotate the shaft back and forth. Continue until the seating area appears universal in texture.

5. Clean the valve carefully to remove all of the abrasive and reinsert.

6. Fit the rubber oil seal on the valve guide.

7. Insert the anchoring dowels with springs attached, to the head by lightly tapping them in place with a pin punch and mallet. The heavier springs should be installed on the intake side.

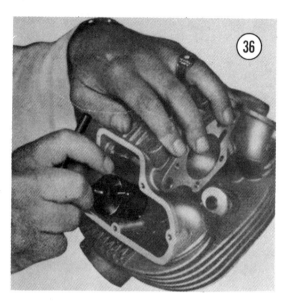

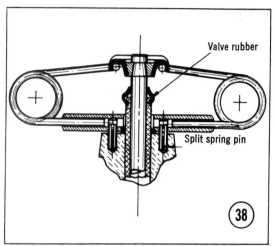

The differences in texture between the cut and worn areas will be obvious.

8. Compress the springs until the spring saddle will fit on the valve stem. See **Figures 37, 38, and 39**.

Camshaft Installation

1. Lubricate the cam lobes with motor oil.
2. Place Woodruff key in its slot on the shaft.
3. Slide bevel gear Z-28 in place.
4. Fit the tab washer in place.
5. Secure the cam and install the left-hand threaded nut.

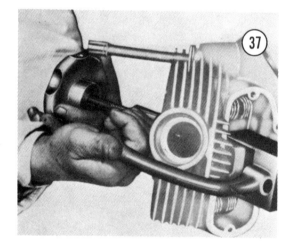

9. Insert the half-cones and release spring pressure.

10. Set the valves by tapping on the stem with a plastic mallet.

Grinding the Valves

If normal lapping doesn't create an effective seal, it will be necessary to regrind the valve seats. This requires the use of the special Ducati tool shown in **Figure 40**. Grind just enough of the seat area to produce an even looking surface.

6. On the opposite side, install the cap and bearing assembly.

7. Install a new drive cover gasket making sure that the oil ducts are clear.

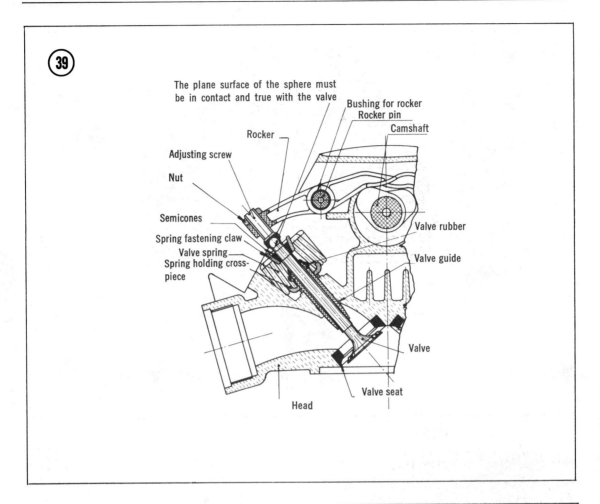

The plane surface of the sphere must
be in contact and true with the valve

Bushing for rocker
Rocker pin
Camshaft

Rocker

Adjusting screw

Nut

Semicones

Spring fastening claw
Valve spring
Spring holding cross-
piece

Valve rubber

Valve guide

Valve

Valve seat

Head

8. Insert the previously assembled drive bearing housing. Align the two bevel gears so that the timing marks coincide as shown in **Figure 41**. The gears should rotate freely without backlash.

9. Shim both gears if the mesh isn't correct.

Rocker Arm Assembly

1. Install the bushing in the rocker and position with shim washers, then insert this assembly in place, as shown in **Figure 42**.

2. Extract the pin slightly and insert a spring washer, as shown in **Figure 43**. The washers should be arranged for the adjusting screw to be positioned on the end of the valve stem, as shown in **Figure 44**.

3. On some 250 models a special adjusting cap must be inserted between the valve and rocker.

4. Place a new gasket on the cap and install.

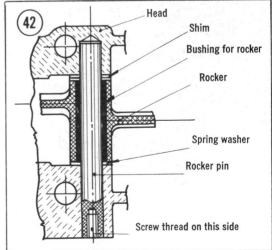

Head

Shim

Bushing for rocker

Rocker

Spring washer

Rocker pin

Screw thread on this side

5. Tap lightly on the cap with a plastic mallet and check the bevel drive positioning.

6. Lock the camshaft securing nut in place by bending the tabs back on the washer.

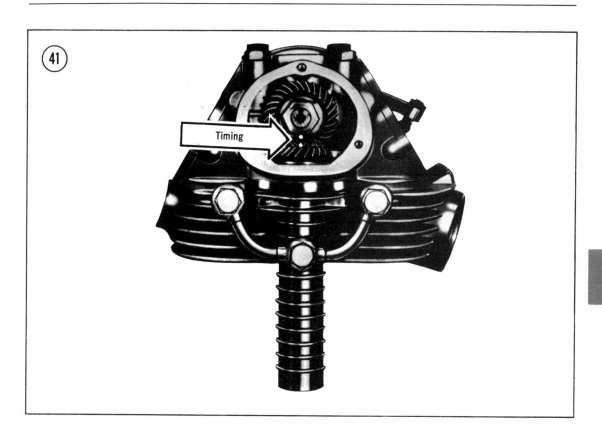

Timing

7. Fit a circlip on the end of the bevel gear shaft at the lower end of the drive cover (**Figure 45**).

Cylinder Head Installation

1. Position the cylinder head over the studs.

2. The system is properly timed if all marks are aligned on the gear (**Figure 46**, page 65).

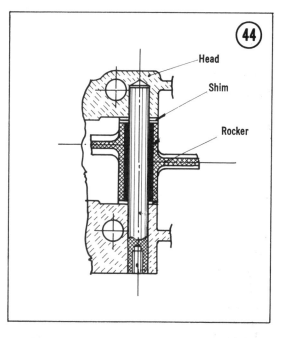

Head

Shim

Rocker

3. The head bolts should be tightened with equal pressure in the sequence in **Figure 47** (page 65). Torque bolts to 250-300 in.-lb. on the 160 series and 300-350 on all other models.

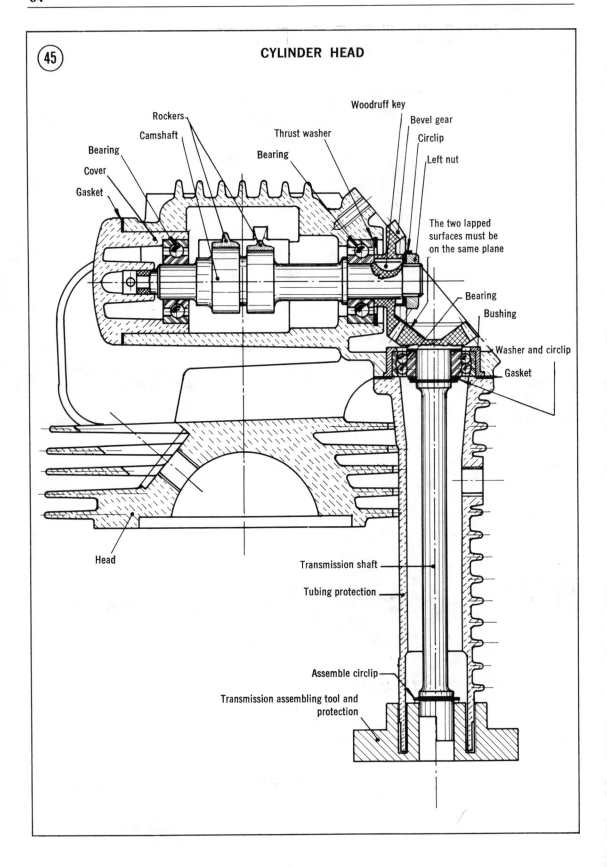

CYLINDER HEAD

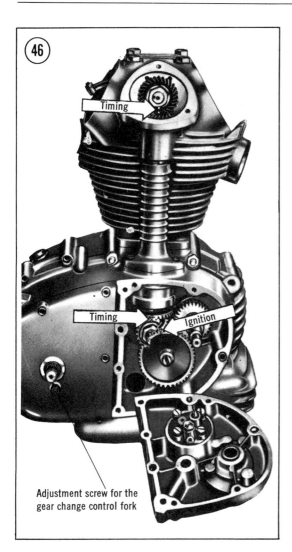

Adjustment screw for the
gear change control fork

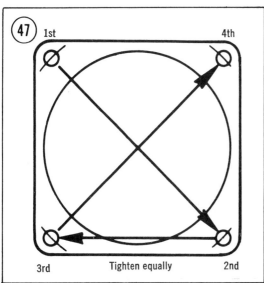

1st · 4th

3rd · Tighten equally · 2nd

Adjusting Valve Timing

1. Remove the threaded plug covering the end of the crankshaft and install a degree wheel as shown in **Figure 48**.

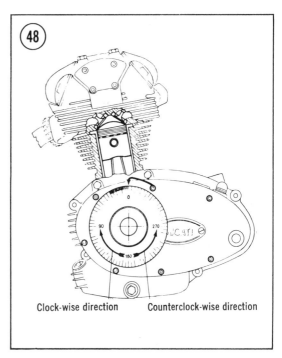

Clock-wise direction   Counterclock-wise direction

2. Fit an indicating needle to one of the cover screws.

3. Rotate the crank until the piston is at top dead center on the compression phase (both valves closed). Set the needle on zero.

4. Adjust the tappets using a feeler gauge and set according to the dimensions given in **Table 1** and as shown in **Figure 49**.

Table 1   VALVE CLEARANCE FIGURES

Model	Intake In. (mm)	Exhaust In. (mm)
160 Monza Jr.	.012 (0.3)	.012 (0.3)
250 Monza	.012 (0.3)	.012 (0.3)
250 GT	.012 (0.3)	.012 (0.3)
250 Mach I	.0098 (0.25)	.016 (0.4)
250 Mark 3	.0098 (0.25)	.016 (0.4)
250 Scrambler	.0098 (0.25)	.012 (0.3)
350 Sebring	.012 (0.3)	.012 (0.3)
450 Mark 3	.0020-.0039 (0.05-0.10) Both valves	
450 Scrambler	.0020-.0039 (0.05-0.10) Both valves	
450 Desmo	.0039-.0059 (0.10-0.15) Both valves	

5. Place a .004 in. (0.1mm) feeler gauge between the intake valve and adjuster.

6. Rotate the crankshaft clockwise until the tappets lock the gauge in place.

7. Read the degree wheel and check that it corresponds to the figures given in **Table 2** for the opening of the intake valve.

8. Continue rotating the crank until the gauge is again free and check the reading of the degree wheel. This should correspond to the value given in Table 2 for the closing of the intake valve.

9. Repeat Steps 5, 6, 7, and 8 for the exhaust valve.

10. If these figures are not correct, check the timing of the gears. The problem could also be caused by excessive clearance near the Woodruff key or by worn rockers or cam lobes.

Final Engine Assembly

Install the following components.

1. Valve covers.

2. Timing system cover.

3. Oil return line.

4. Intake manifold gasket.

5. Carburetor spacer.

6. Intake manifold.

7. Carburetor.

8. Pedal return spring and adjusting plate in their housing.

9. Locating studs.

10. Spring and ball.

11. Gear shift lever.

12. Gear selector control fork in selector collar

Table 2   IGNITION TIMING

Model	Intake		Exhaust	
	Opens ±5°	Closes ±5°	Opens ±5°	Closes ±5°
160 Monza Junior	24°	40°	51°	30°
250 Monza and GT from eng. No. 87422	20°	70°	50°	30°
250 GT up to eng. No. 87421	52°	52°	75°	27°
250 Mark 3, 1964	62°	68°	75°	55°
250 Mach 1 & Mark 3, 1965-1966	62°	76°	70°	48°
250 SCR	30°	84°	63°	38°
250 Scrambler	32°	75°	55°	44°
350 Sebring	20°	70°	50°	30°
450 Mark 3	60°	75°	75°	45°
450 SCR	27°	75°	60°	32°

(**Figure 50**). Position the fork to the first two selector pins (counting left to right). See **Figure 51**.

13. Fork thrust spring and thrust washer on the fork control spindle.

14. Selector cover.

15. Check the operation of the gearshift selector. Adjust, if necessary, with the eccentric screw and locknut.

16. The chain and gearbox side cover is fitted after the engine is in the frame.

17. Reverse the sequence of *Engine Removal* to install the engine in the frame.

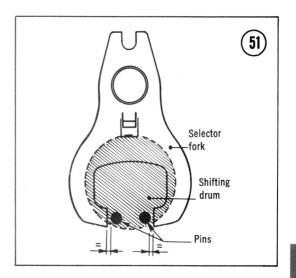

Selector fork

Shifting drum

Pins

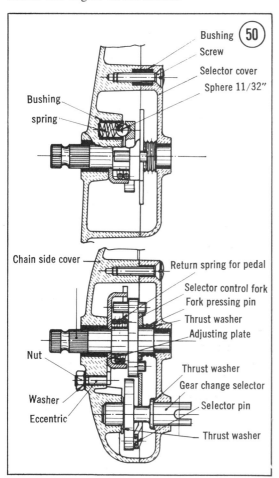

Bushing 50
Screw
Selector cover
Sphere 11/32"

Bushing
spring

Chain side cover
Return spring for pedal
Selector control fork
Fork pressing pin
Thrust washer
Adjusting plate

Nut

Thrust washer
Gear change selector

Washer
Eccentric
Selector pin
Thrust washer

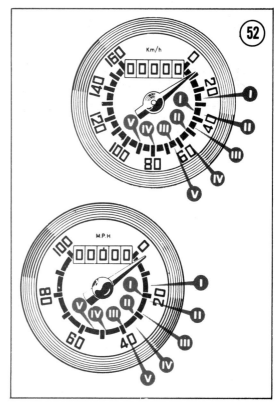

Breaking In a Rebuilt Engine

A rebuilt engine requires the same care and break-in as a new engine since most of the parts are new. Follow the shift points as shown in **Figure 52**. Never over-rev or allow the engine to labor at low speeds. Change the oil after 300-500 miles and clean the oil filter. New parts shed the scraps of metal which are left after machining operations.

Check valve and ignition timing after the initial break-in period and tighten all nuts and bolts. If these few simple precautions are followed, your Ducati should be good for many more trouble-free miles.

CHAPTER FIVE

CARBURETION

For proper operation, a gasoline engine must be supplied with fuel and air, mixed in the proper proportions by weight. A mixture in which there is an excess of fuel is said to be rich. A lean mixture is one which contains insufficient fuel. It is the function of the carburetor to supply the proper mixture to the engine under all operating conditions.

Ducati motorcycles are equipped with Amal, or Dellorto carburetors. Service procedures are similar for the two. Differences are pointed out where they exist. Carburetors may be of either monobloc (**Figure 1**) or concentric (**Figure 2**) type.

CARBURETOR OPERATION

Figure 3 (pages 70-71) is an exploded view of a typical carburetor. The essential functional parts are a float and float valve mechanism for maintaining a constant fuel level in the float bowl, a pilot system for supplying fuel at low speeds, a main fuel system which supplies the engine at medium and high speeds, and a tickler system, which supplies the very rich mixture needed to start a cold engine. The operation of each system is discussed in the following paragraphs.

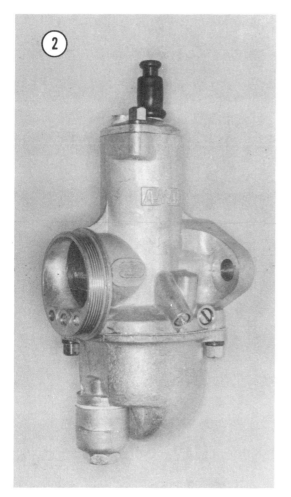

Float Mechanism

Figure 4 illustrates a typical float mechanism. Proper operation of the carburetor is dependent on maintaining a constant fuel level in the carburetor bowl. As fuel is drawn from the float bowl, the float level drops. When the float drops, the float valve moves away from its seat and allows fuel to flow past the valve and seat into the float bowl. As this occurs, the float is then raised, pressing the valve against its seat, thereby shutting off the flow of fuel. It can be seen from this discussion that a small piece of dirt can be trapped between the valve and seat, preventing the valve from closing and allowing fuel to rise beyond the normal level, resulting in flooding. **Figures 5A and 5B** illustrate this condition.

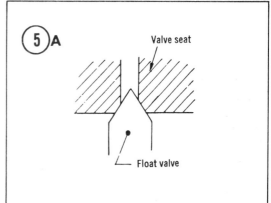

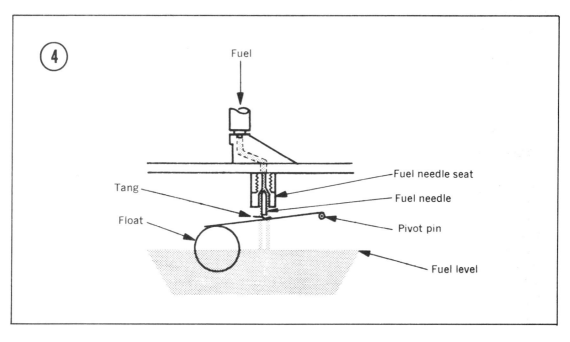

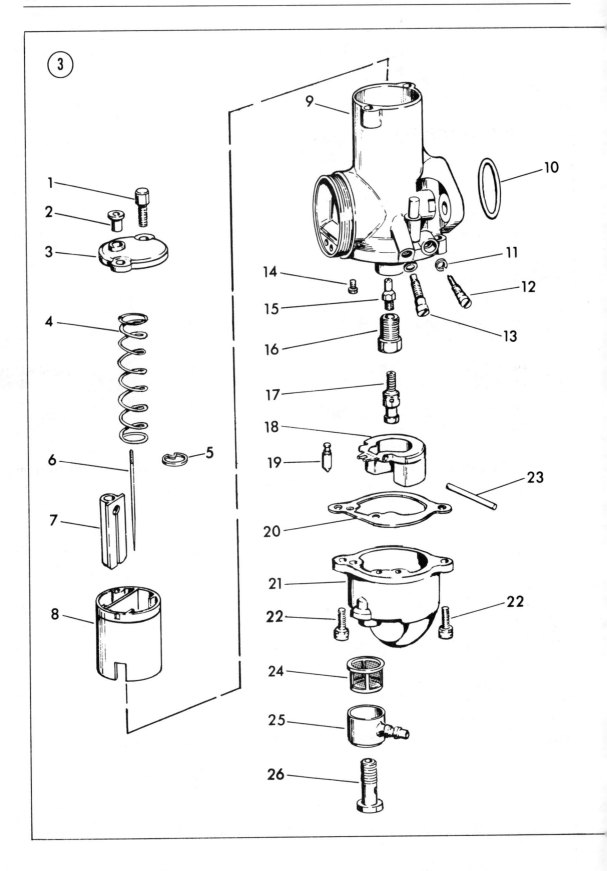

AMAL CARBURETOR

1. Screw
2. Ferrule
3. Mixing chamber cap
4. Spring
5. Jet needle clip
6. Jet needle
7. Choke valve
8. Throttle valve
9. Mixing chamber body
10. O-ring
11. O-ring
12. Pilot air screw
13. Throttle stop screw
14. Pilot jet
15. Needle jet
16. Jet holder
17. Main jet
18. Float
19. Float needle
20. Gasket
21. Float bowl
22. Screw
23. Float pivot
24. Filter screen
25. Banjo
26. Banjo bolt

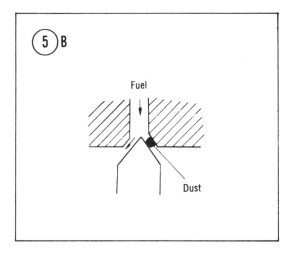

Pilot System

Under idle or low speed conditions, at less than one-eighth throttle, the engine doesn't require much fuel or air, and the throttle valve is almost closed. A separate pilot system is required for operation under such conditions. **Figure 6** illustrates the operation of the pilot system. Air is drawn through the pilot air inlet and controlled by the pilot air screw. The air is then mixed with fuel drawn through the pilot jet. The air/fuel mixture then travels from the pilot outlet into the main air passage, where it is further mixed with air prior to being drawn into the engine. The pilot air screw controls the idle mixture.

If proper idle and low speed mixture cannot be obtained within the normal adjustment range of the idle mixture screw, refer to **Table 1** for possible causes.

Table 1   IDLE MIXTURE

Too rich
Clogged pilot air intake Clogged air passage Clogged air bleed opening Pilot jet loose
Too lean
Obstructed pilot jet Obstructed jet outlet Worn throttle valve Carburetor mounting loose

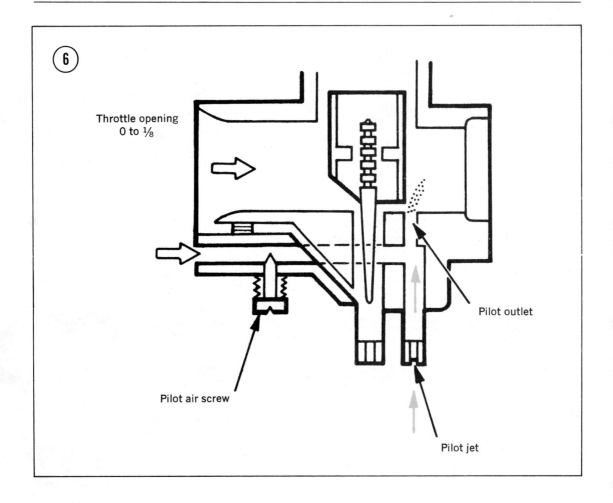

Throttle opening
0 to ⅛

Pilot outlet

Pilot air screw

Pilot jet

Main Fuel System

As the throttle is opened still more, up to about one-quarter open, the pilot circuit begins to supply less of the mixture to the engine, as the main fuel system, illustrated in **Figure 7**, begins to function. The main jet, the needle jet, the jet needle, and the air jet make up the main fuel circuit.

As the throttle valve opens more than about one-eighth of its travel, air is drawn through the main port, and passes under the throttle valve in the main bore. The velocity of the air stream results in reduced pressure around the jet needle. Fuel then passes through the main jet, past the needle jet and jet needle, and into the air stream where it is atomized and sent to the cylinder. As the throttle valve opens, more air flows through the carburetor. The jet needle, which is attached to the throttle slide, rises to permit more fuel to flow.

A portion of the air bled past the air jet passes through the needle jet bleed air inlet into the needle jet, where the air is mixed with the main air stream and atomized.

Airflow at small throttle openings is controlled primarily by the cutaway on the throttle slide.

As the throttle is opened wider, up to about three-quarters open, the circuit draws air from two sources, as shown in **Figure 8**. The first source is air passing through the venturi; the second source is through the air jet. Air passing through the venturi draws fuel through the needle jet. The jet needle is tapered, and therefore allows more fuel to pass. Air passing through the air jet passes to the needle jet to aid atomization of the fuel there.

Figure 9 illustrates the circuit at high speeds. The jet needle is withdrawn almost completely from the needle jet. Fuel flow is then controlled by the main jet. Air passing through the air jet

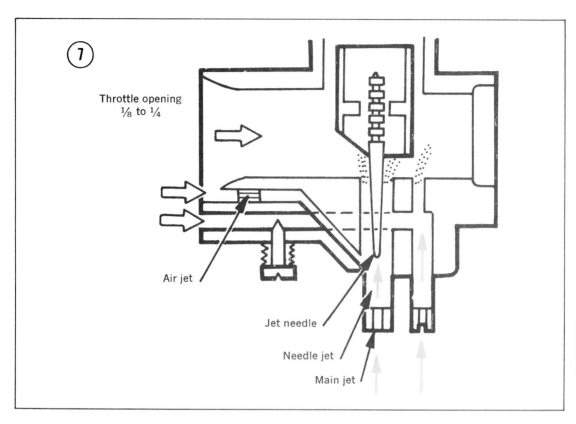

7

Throttle opening
⅛ to ¼

Air jet

Jet needle

Needle jet

Main jet

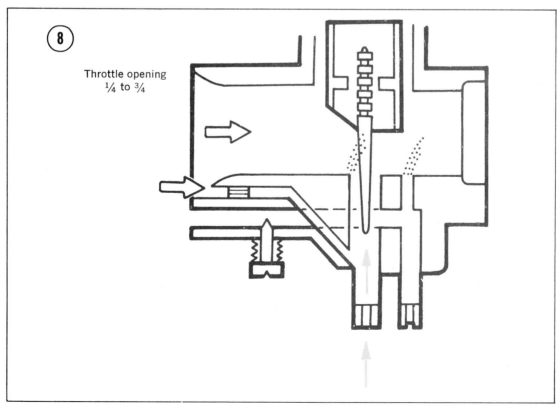

8

Throttle opening
¼ to ¾

5

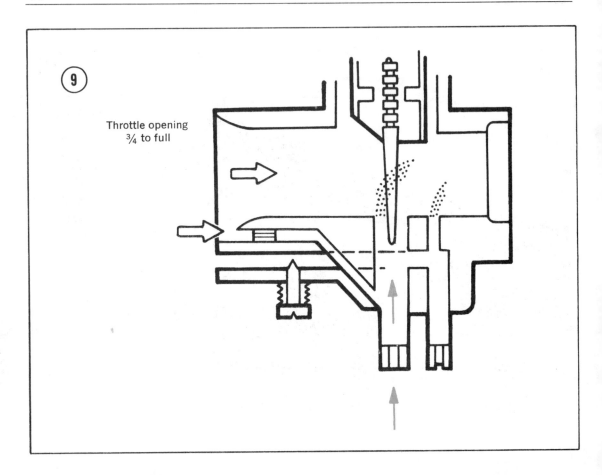

⑨

Throttle opening
¾ to full

continues to aid atomization of the fuel as described in the foregoing paragraphs.

Any dirt which collects in the main jet or in the needle jet obstructs fuel flow and causes a lean mixture. Any clogged air passage, such as the air bleed opening or air jet, may result in an overrich mixture. Other causes of a rich mixture are a worn needle jet, loose needle jet, or loose main jet. If the jet needle is worn, it should be replaced. However, it may be possible to effect a temporary repair by placing the needle jet clip in a higher groove.

Tickler System

A cold engine requires a mixture which is far richer than normal. The tickler system provides this rich mixture. When the rider presses the tickler button, the float is forced downward, causing the float needle valve to open, and thereby allowing extra fuel to flow into the float chamber.

CARBURETOR OVERHAUL

There is no set rule regarding frequency of carburetor overhaul. A carburetor used primarily for street riding may go 5,000 miles without attention. If the bike is used in dirt, the carburetor might need an overhaul in less than 1,000 miles. Poor engine performance, hesitation, and little response to idle mixture adjustment are all symptoms of possible carburetor malfunctions. As a general rule, it is good practice to overhaul the carburetor each time you perform a routine decarbonization of the engine.

Concentric Bowl Carburetor Disassembly

1. Remove the mixing chamber cap (**Figure 10**) if this step has not been performed previously.
2. Withdraw the throttle valve (**Figure 11**). Don't lose the spring or spring plate. Note the position of each part as it is removed.

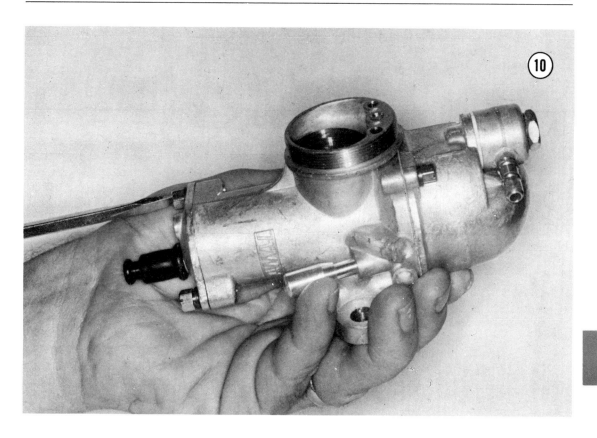

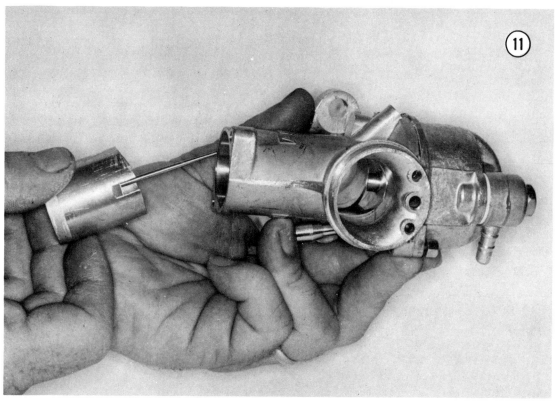

3. Remove the float bowl (**Figure 12**).

4. Remove the float and float needle together (**Figure 13**).

5. Remove the banjo bolt (**Figure 14**), then the fuel inlet banjo fitting (**Figure 15**).

6. Carefully remove the filter screen (**Figure 16**). Do not crush the screen as you remove it.

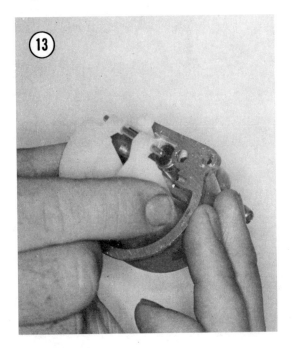

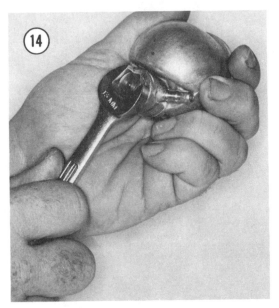

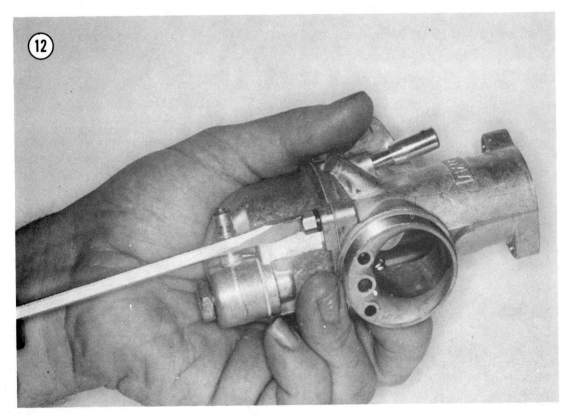

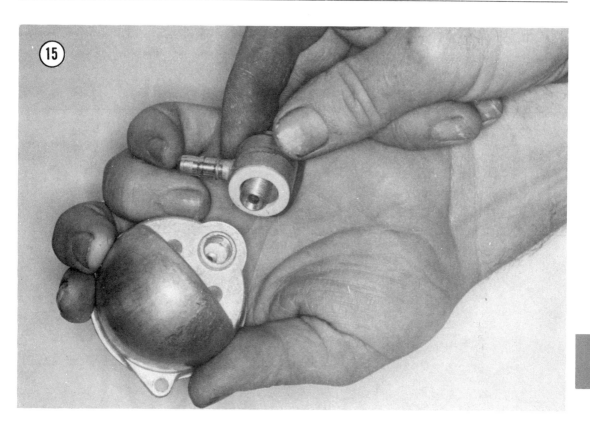

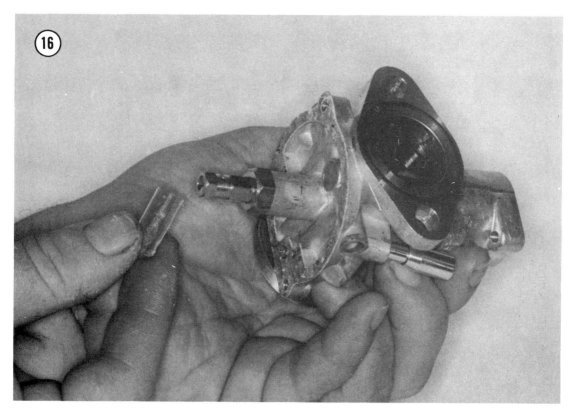

7. Remove the main jet (**Figure 17**).

8. Remove the jet holder (**Figure 18**). Unscrew the needle jet from the jet holder if necessary.

9. Remove the pilot jet (**Figure 19**).

10. Remove the mounting flange O-ring.

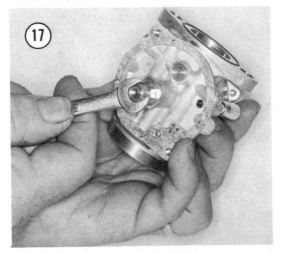

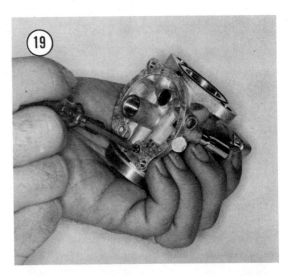

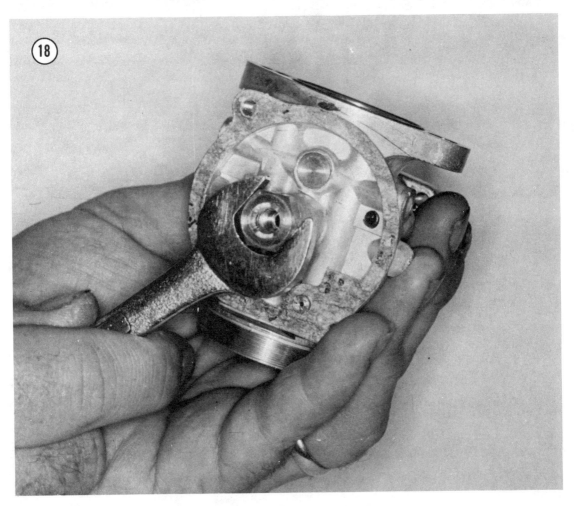

11. Remove pilot air screw, throttle stop screw, and tickler assembly.

12. Reverse the disassembly procedure to reassemble the carburetor. Always use new gaskets upon reassembly.

Amal Monobloc Carburetor
Disassembly

Figure 20 (next page) is an exploded view of a typical Monobloc carburetor. Refer to this illustration during carburetor disassembly.

1. Remove the top ring nut (**Figure 21**).

2. Remove the throttle slide assembly. See **Figure 22**.

3. Note which jet needle groove the clip is in, then remove the jet needle clip and pull the jet needle from the throttle valve.

4. Remove the float chamber cover (**Figure 23**).

5. Remove the spacer from the float pivot shaft (**Figure 24**). Note the manner in which the float is installed, then pull it from the pivot shaft (**Figure 25**).

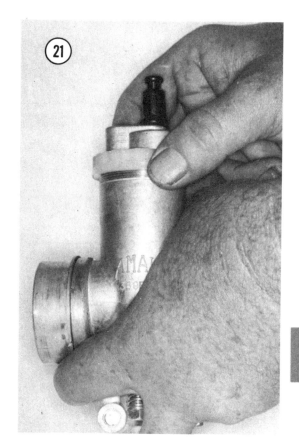

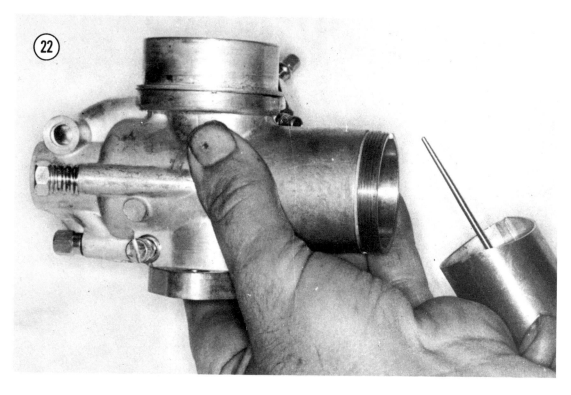

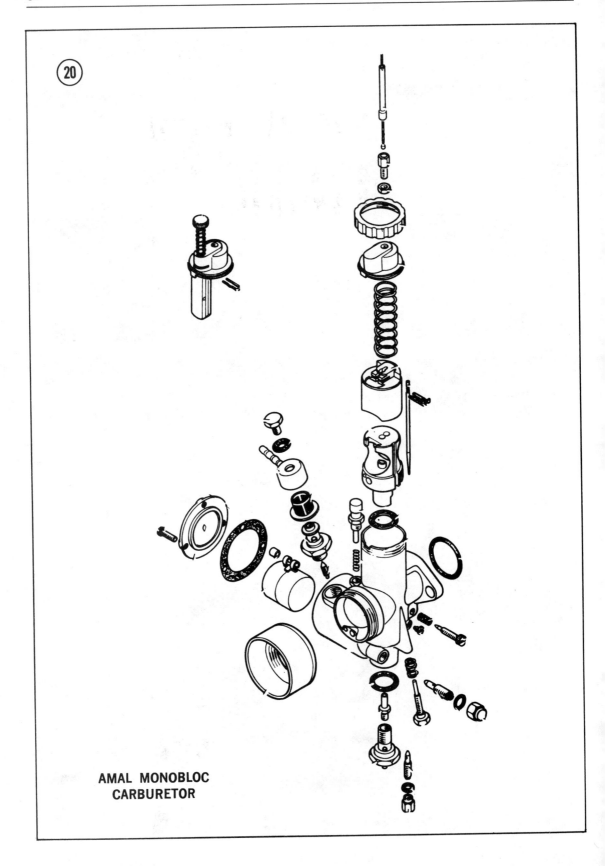

AMAL MONOBLOC
CARBURETOR

5

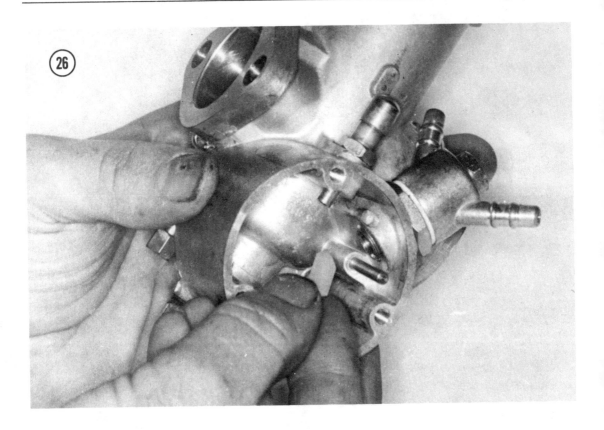

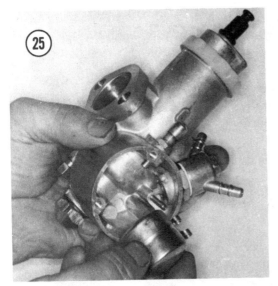

9. Separate the needle jet from the jet holder (**Figure 30**).

10. Remove the pilot jet cover (**Figure 31**), then the pilot jet (**Figure 32**).

6. Remove the float needle (**Figure 26**), then the float needle seat.

7. Remove the main jet cover (**Figure 27**), then remove the main jet together with its gasket (**Figure 28**).

8. Remove the jet holder (**Figure 29**).

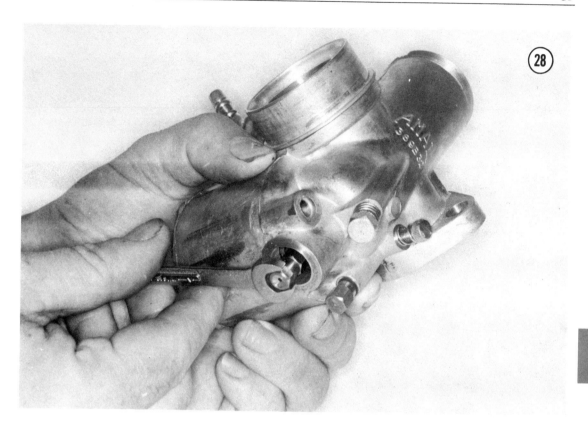

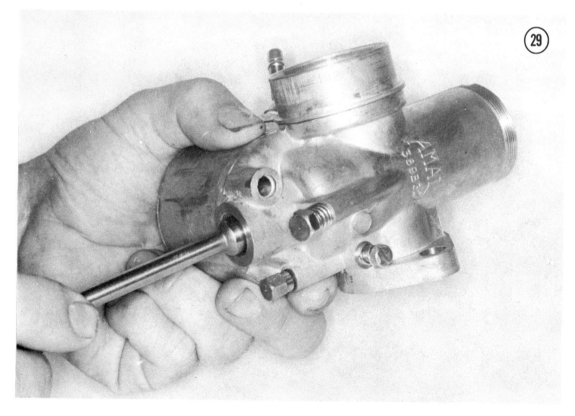

5

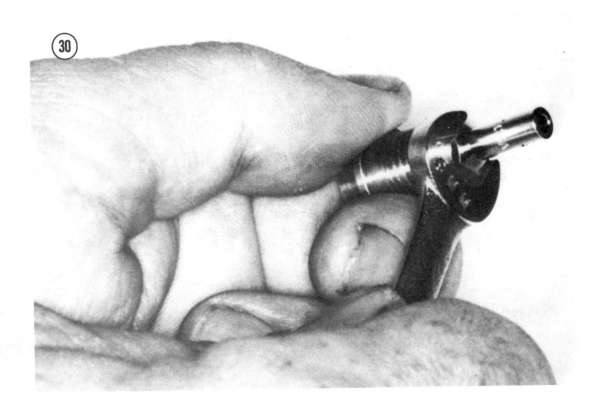

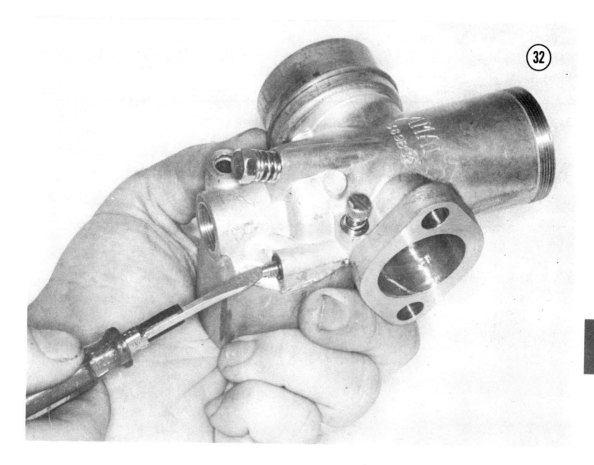

11. Remove the banjo bolt, then the fuel inlet fitting (**Figure 33**).

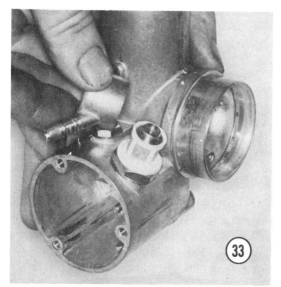

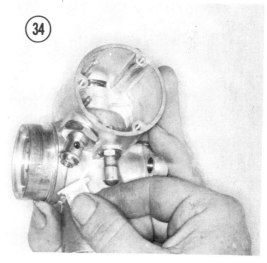

12. Remove the fuel strainer (**Figure 34**), then the float needle seat.

13. Remove the pilot air screw, tickler button, and throttle stop screw.

14. Reverse the disassembly procedure to reassemble the carburetor. Always use new gaskets upon reassembly.

CARBURETOR ADJUSTMENT

Carburetor adjustment is not normally required except for occasional adjustment of idling speed, or at time of carburetor overhaul.

Float Level

The machine was delivered with the float level adjusted correctly. Floats on Ducati carburetors do not have provision for adjustment.

Float Inspection

Shake the float to check for gasoline inside (**Figure 35**). If fuel leaks into the float, the float chamber fuel level will rise, resulting in an over-rich mixture. Replace the float if it is deformed or leaking.

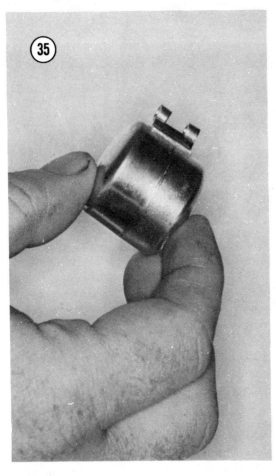

Replace the float valve if its seating end is scratched or worn. Press the float valve gently with your finger and make sure that the valve seats properly. If the float valve does not seat properly, fuel will overflow, causing a rich mixture and flooding the float chamber whenever the fuel petcock is open.

Clean all parts in carburetor cleaning solvent. Dry the parts with compressed air. Clean the jets and other delicate parts with compressed air after the float bowl has been removed. Never attempt to clean jets or passages by running a wire through them. To do so will cause damage and destroy their calibration. Do not use compressed air to clean an assembled carburetor, since the float and float valve can be damaged.

Speed Range Adjustments

The carburetor on your machine was designed to provide the proper mixture under all operating conditions. Little or no benefit will result from experimenting. However, unusual operating conditions such as sustained operation at high altitudes or unusually high or low temperatures may make modifications to the standard specifications desirable. The adjustments described in the following paragraphs should only be undertaken if the rider has definite reason to believe they are required. Make the tests and adjustments in the order specified.

Figure 36 illustrates typical carburetor components which may be changed to meet individual operating conditions. Shown left to right are the main jet, needle jet, jet needle and clip, and throttle valve.

Make a road test at full throttle for final determination of main jet size. To make such a test, operate the motorcycle at full throttle for at least two minutes, then shut the engine off, release the clutch, and stop the bike.

If at full throttle, the engine runs "heavily," the main jet is too large. If the engine runs better by closing the throttle slightly, the main jet is too small. The engine will run evenly at full throttle if the main jet is of the correct size.

After each such test, remove and examine the spark plug. The insulator should have a light tan color. If the insulator has black sooty deposits, the mixture is too rich. If there are signs of intense heat, such as a blistered white appearance, the mixture is too lean.

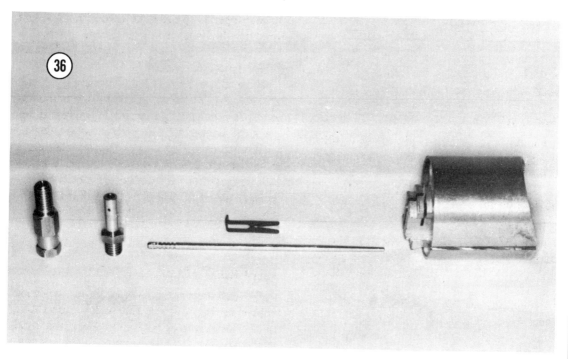

As a general rule, main jet size should be reduced approximately five percent for each 3,000 feet (1,000 meters) above sea level.

Table 2 lists symptoms caused by rich and lean mixtures.

Table 2   **CARBURETOR MIXTURE**

Condition	Symptom
Rich Mixture	Rough Idle Black exhaust smoke Hard starting, especially when hot "Blubbering" under acceleration Black deposits in exhaust pipe Gas-fouled spark plug Poor gas mileage Engine performs worse as it warms up
Lean Mixture	Backfiring Rough idle Overheating Hesitation upon acceleration Engine speed varies at fixed throttle Loss of power White color on spark plug insulator Poor acceleration

Adjust the pilot screw as follows.

1. Turn the pilot air screw in until it seats lightly, then back it out about 1½ turns.

2. Start the engine and warm it to normal operating temperature.

3. Turn the idle speed screw until the engine runs slower and begins to falter.

4. Adjust the pilot screw as required to make the engine run smoothly.

5. Repeat Steps 3 and 4 to achieve the lowest stable idle speed.

Next, determine the proper throttle valve cutaway size. With the engine running at idle, open the throttle. If the engine does not accelerate smoothly from idle, turn the pilot air screw in (clockwise) slightly to richen the mixture. If the condition still exists, return the air screw to its original position and replace the throttle valve with one which has a smaller cutaway. If engine operation is reduced by turning the air screw, replace the throttle valve with one having a larger cutaway.

For operation at ¼ to ¾ throttle opening, adjustment is made with the jet needle. Operate the engine at half throttle in a manner similar to that for full throttle tests described earlier. To enrich the mixture, place the jet needle clip in a lower groove. Conversely, placing the clip in a higher groove leans the mixture.

A summary of carburetor adjustments is given in **Table 3**.

Table 3   CARBURETOR ADJUSTMENTS

Throttle Opening	Adjustment	If too Rich	If too Lean
0 - 1/8	Air screw	Turn out	Turn in
1/8 - 1/4	Throttle valve cutaway	Use larger cutaway	Use smaller cutaway
1/4 - 3/4	Jet needle	Raise clip	Lower clip
3/4 - full	Main jet	Use smaller number	Use larger number

DELLORTO CARBURETOR DISASSEMBLY

The procedures outlined for the disassembly of an Amal carburetor can be applied with success on the Dellorto series. The procedures for tuning, inspection, and repair also apply. Check **Figure 37** carefully for the location of all components prior to starting work.

Air Filter

Most Ducati motorcycles come equipped with paper filters. These can't be cleaned but excess dirt can be shaken out at frequent intervals.

Accessory houses have wet foam filters, made to fit any bike, which are more efficient and can be cleaned in kerosene. Allow the filter to air dry and dip in lightweight oil. Squeeze out excess oil and insert in the stock housing.

Dirt riding will make it necessary to check the filter after every ride. Even minute particles of dust can cause severe wear so never run without a filter.

DELLORTO CARBURETOR

1. Screw
2. Catch
3. Idler jet
4. Gasket
5. Nut
6. Starter valve
7. Plug
8. Gasket
9. Filtering body
10. Hexagon nut
11. Chamber body
12. Throttle cover
13. Float pin
14. Stud
15. Gasket
16. Spring
17. Spring
18. Spring
19. Screw
20. Float
21. Gasket
22. Insulator
23. Throttle valve
24. Taper needle
25. Spring
26. Cap
27. Washer
28. Screw
29. Fuel closing pin
30. Suction pipe
31. Fuel filter
32. Cover
33. Ring
34. Gasket
35. Screw
36. Air intake bell
37. Carburetor
38. Screw
39. Starter jet
40. Main jet
41. Screw nut
42. Pipe
43. Atomizer
44. Screw

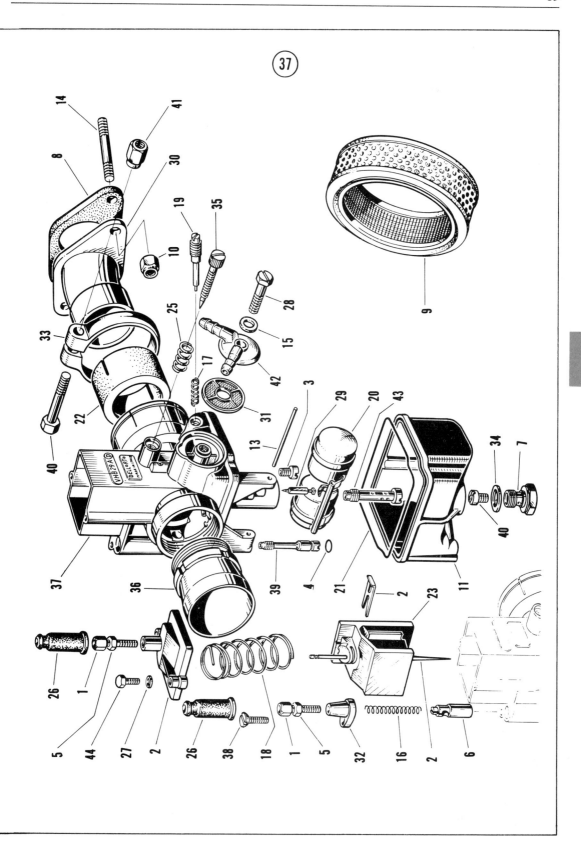

CHAPTER SIX

CHASSIS

Complete dismantling is seldom necessary unless the frame has been damaged in an accident or through rough abuse in competition. Most critical assemblies can be removed for repair or left on the machine for adjustment.

The procedure for dismantling continues where the section on *Engine Removal* left off in Chapter Four.

Handlebars

1. Disconnect all wires at the junction farthest from the bars. Almost all wires are color coded (see Chapter Three for specifics) but old age may have caused them to fade beyond recognition. If the colors aren't discernible, mark with masking tape and a felt tip pen to simplify reassembly.

2. Pull the clutch cable, loosen the adjusting screw, then remove from the lever.

3. Loosen the front brake adjuster, then remove the cable end from the lever. The cable may be left with the front wheel assembly.

4. Remove the starter lever, choke, or compression release cables, if the bike is so equipped.

5. Remove the screws on the body of the throttle twist grip and rotate the housing until the cable can be removed.

6. Remove the handlebar clamp bolts, then lift off the bar.

7. Replace the bar or straighten if bent.

8. Check the cables and housing and lube with graphite.

9. Reverse the previous steps for reassembly. The clutch, front brake and throttle cables should be adjusted to include a little play before actuating. The throttle, for instance, should not be set up without any play or the bike will accelerate when the handlebars are turned.

Front Forks

1. **Figure 1** is an exploded view of a typical Ducati fork and steering dampener. Service procedures are similar for most models.

2. Remove the front axle pinch bolts at the base of each fork tube.

3. Disconnect the speedometer cable.

4. Disconnect the front brake cable.

5. Lift the front end and support the engine on a box or suitable stand.

6. Pull out the front axle and remove the wheel. On some models it may be necessary to remove the fender first.

7. Loosen the lower steering yoke fork clamp bolts (38) if either of the fork tubes are to be removed separately.

8. Remove the upper yoke sealing plugs (6). These plugs also secure the fork tubes.

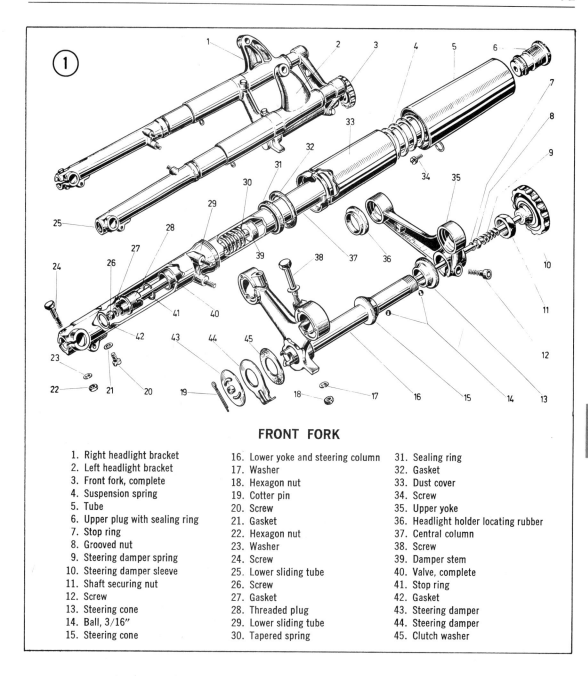

FRONT FORK

1. Right headlight bracket
2. Left headlight bracket
3. Front fork, complete
4. Suspension spring
5. Tube
6. Upper plug with sealing ring
7. Stop ring
8. Grooved nut
9. Steering damper spring
10. Steering damper sleeve
11. Shaft securing nut
12. Screw
13. Steering cone
14. Ball, 3/16″
15. Steering cone

16. Lower yoke and steering column
17. Washer
18. Hexagon nut
19. Cotter pin
20. Screw
21. Gasket
22. Hexagon nut
23. Washer
24. Screw
25. Lower sliding tube
26. Screw
27. Gasket
28. Threaded plug
29. Lower sliding tube
30. Tapered spring

31. Sealing ring
32. Gasket
33. Dust cover
34. Screw
35. Upper yoke
36. Headlight holder locating rubber
37. Central column
38. Screw
39. Damper stem
40. Valve, complete
41. Stop ring
42. Gasket
43. Steering damper
44. Steering damper
45. Clutch washer

9. Slide the fork tube downward to remove.

10. Both fork tubes may be removed as described, or as a unit, with the lower yoke and steering column.

11. To remove the entire front end, remove the cotter pin (19) at the bottom of the steering column.

12. Next, remove the steering dampener components (43, 44, 45).

13. Loosen the shaft securing nut (11) and slide out the shaft (10).

14. Place a pan directly under the two yokes and remove the fork assembly. Be careful that none of the ball bearings are lost.

15. Clean the balls and races with kerosene to remove all of the old grease and dirt. Use heavy grease to hold the bearings in place during assembly. To assemble, reverse procedures.

Fork Tube Dismantling and Assembly

The procedure for assembling the Ducati forks is difficult to explain but disassembly is relatively easy. For this reason, we will show assembly only. Reverse the procedure to dismantle.

1. Insert the nine balls in the valve seat (40) and hold in place with heavy grease. Close the assembly with the washer and place on the support as shown in **Figure 2**.

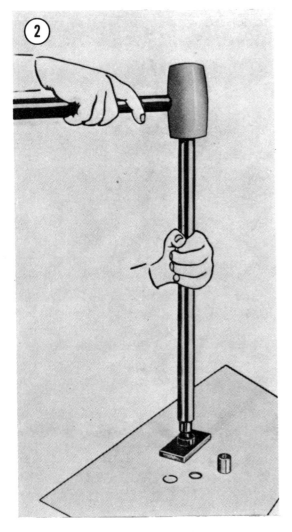

2. Wash the central column (37) with naptha and a small brush. Fit it into place by tapping on the end of the tube with a rubber or leather mallet. Lock with the stop ring (41).

3. Next, insert the washer (42) into the threaded plug (28) and smear the threads with jointing compound.

4. Screw plug into lower sliding tube (25). See **Figure 3**.

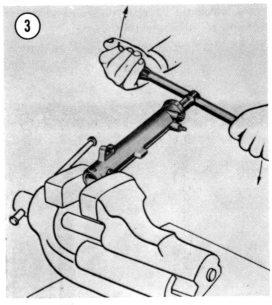

5. Secure the screw (20) in its hole with the gasket (21).

6. Install the sealing ring (31) using a punch as shown in **Figure 4**.

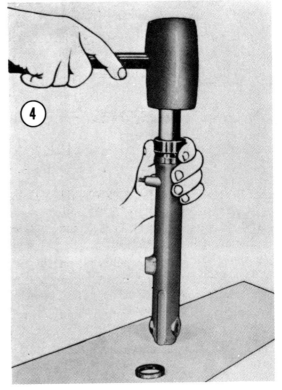

7. Insert central column (37) and gasket (32) into the lower sliding tube (25).

8. Lubricate the threads with grease and install the dust cover (33) with its washer.

9. Insert the guide bushing as shown in **Figure 5**.

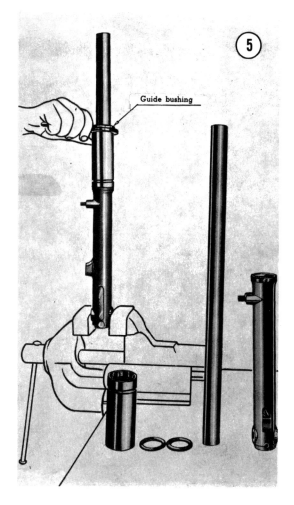

10. Install the lower steering cone (15) on the steering column and lower yoke (16).

11. Install bolt (38), washer (17), and nut (18), but do not tighten completely.

12. Place the two upper tubes (5) on the yoke as shown in **Figure 6** and insert the screws using a magnetic screwdriver.

13. Insert the spring (30) into the tube (37) and onto the damper stem (39).

14. Apply tension on the stem while securing with the screw (26) and washer (27) as shown in **Figure 7**.

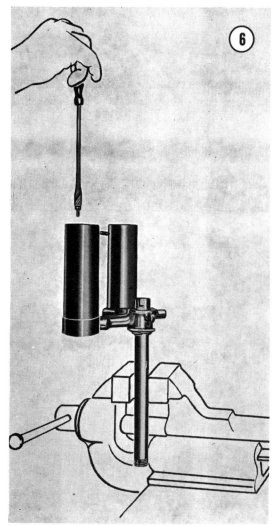

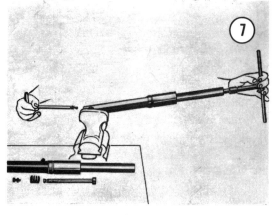

15. Extract the tube and lubricate with grease. Insert the suspension spring (4) and install the lower yoke (16). See **Figure 8**.

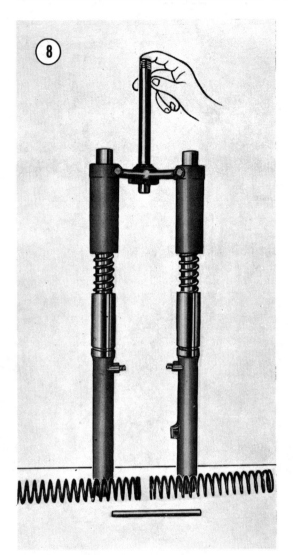

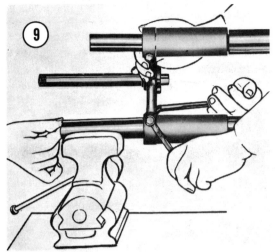

22. Insert the upper plug (6) and sealing ring as shown in **Figure 10**.

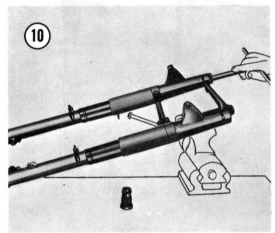

16. Grip the central column in a vise and pull on shaft plate until it is 6 in. (157mm) long.

17. Someone will have to tighten the screw (38) while holding the nut (18) firm, as shown in **Figure 9**.

18. Repeat the previous operations for the other fork leg.

19. Install headlight mounting brackets (1, 2) and the two rubber spacers (36).

20. The upper yoke (35), balls (14), box (13), plug (6) and steering dampener parts are installed when the forks are being fitted to the frame.

21. Fill the fork legs with the quality of oil mentioned in the table on page 106.

Wheel Inspection

1. Grasp two consecutive spokes and squeeze. If they move, tension is not sufficient. Another method for checking is to rap the individual spokes with a wrench or key. A properly tuned spoke will produce a clean ringing sound. A loose spoke will produce a dull thud.

2. Tighten each loose spoke one quarter of a turn at the nipple working around the wheel until all are tight. Tightening each spoke fully at first will cause the wheel to be out-of-round.

Wheel Balancing

1. The wheels must revolve freely to balance them properly. Loosen the axle nuts and remove the rear chain to eliminate friction.

2. Spin the wheel and let it coast to a stop. Mark the top of the wheel with a piece of chalk. Repeat several times to ensure that this spot is the lightest. A perfectly balanced wheel will stop in random spots.

3. Weights are available to attach to the spokes where the wheel needs balancing. See **Figure 11**. After adding each weight, spin the wheel and proceed as indicated in Steps 1 and 2.

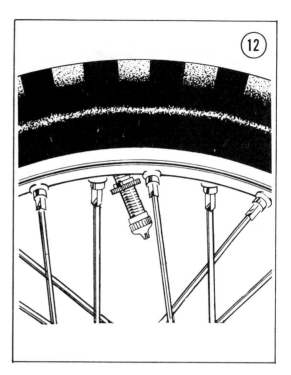

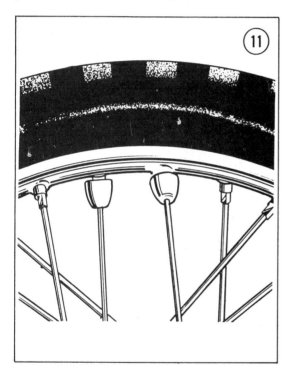

4. Check the tightness of the valve stem. A loose stem, as shown in **Figure 12**, can shift and be torn loose causing the tire to deflate.

Wheel Alignment

1. Measure the width of the two tires at their widest points.

2. Subtract the smaller dimension from the larger.

3. Nail a piece of wood, equal to the figure obtained in Step 2, to a straight piece of wood approximately 7 feet long. See **Figure 13** (D).

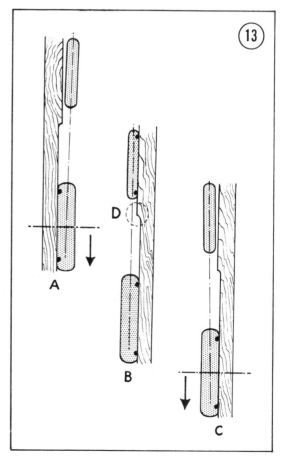

4. Lay the straight edge on blocks six inches high and place against the tires. If the wheels are aligned, the board will touch each wheel at two points as shown in (B) Figure 13.

5. If the wheels are not aligned as in (A) and (C), Figure 13, the rear wheel must be shifted to correct the situation. The chain adjuster must cause the wheel to move toward the rear on the side shown for the error indicated in Figure 13.

6. If the frame has been bent, this may not correct the misalignment. Replace the frame or have it aligned by an expert.

TIRE CHANGING AND REPAIR

1. Remove the valve core to deflate the tire.

2. Press the entire bead on both sides of the tire into the center of the rim.

3. Lubricate the beads with soapy water.

4. Insert the tire iron under the bead next to the valve. Force the bead on the opposite side of the tire into the center of the rim and pry the bead over the rim with the tire iron (see **Figure 14**).

5. Insert a second tire iron next to the first to hold the bead over the rim. Then work around the tire with the first tire iron, prying the bead over the rim (see **Figure 15**). Be careful not to pinch the inner tube with the tire irons.

6. Remove the valve from the hole in the rim and remove the tube from the tire. Lift out and lay aside.

7. Stand the tire upright. Insert a tire iron between the second bead and the side of the rim that the first bead was pryed over (see **Figure 16**). Force the bead on the opposite side from the tire iron into the center of the rim. Pry the second bead off the rim, working around as with the first.

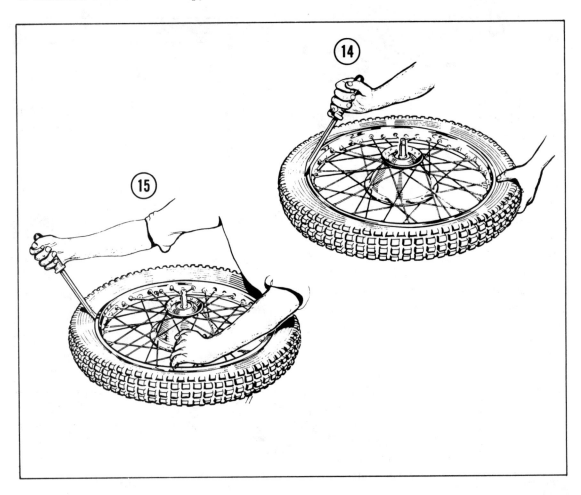

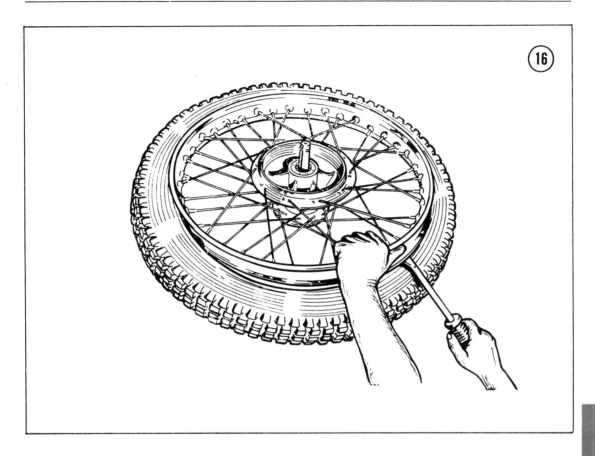

Tire Replacement

1. Carefully check the tire for any damage, especially inside.

2. A new tire may have balancing rubbers inside. These are not patches and should not be disturbed. A white spot near the bead indicates a lighter point on the tire. This should be placed next to the valve or midway between the two rim locks if they are installed.

3. Check that the spoke ends do not protrude through the nipples into the center of the rim to puncture the tube. File off any protruding spoke ends.

4. Be sure the rim rubber tape is in place with the rough side toward the rim.

5. Put the core in the tube valve. Put the tube in the tire and inflate just enough to round it out. Too much air will make installing the tire difficult, and too little will increase the chances of pinching the tube with the tire irons.

6. Lubricate the tire beads and rim with soapy water. Pull the tube partly out of the tire at the valve. Squeeze the beads together to hold the tube and insert the valve into the hole in the rim (see **Figure 17**). The lower bead should go into the center of the rim with the upper bead outside it.

7. Press the lower bead into the rim center on each side of the valve, working around the tire in both directions (see **Figure 18**). Use a tire iron for the last few inches of bead (see **Figure 19**).

8. Press the upper bead into the rim opposite the valve. Pry the bead into the rim on both sides of the initial point with a tire iron, working around the rim to the valve (see **Figure 20**).

9. Wiggle the valve to be sure the tube is not trapped under the bead. Set the valve squarely in its hole before screwing on the valve nut to hold it against the rim.

10. Check the bead on both sides of the tire for even fit around the rim. Inflate the tire slowly to seat the beads in the rim. It may be necessary to bounce the tire to complete the seating. Inflate to the required pressure. Balance the wheel as described.

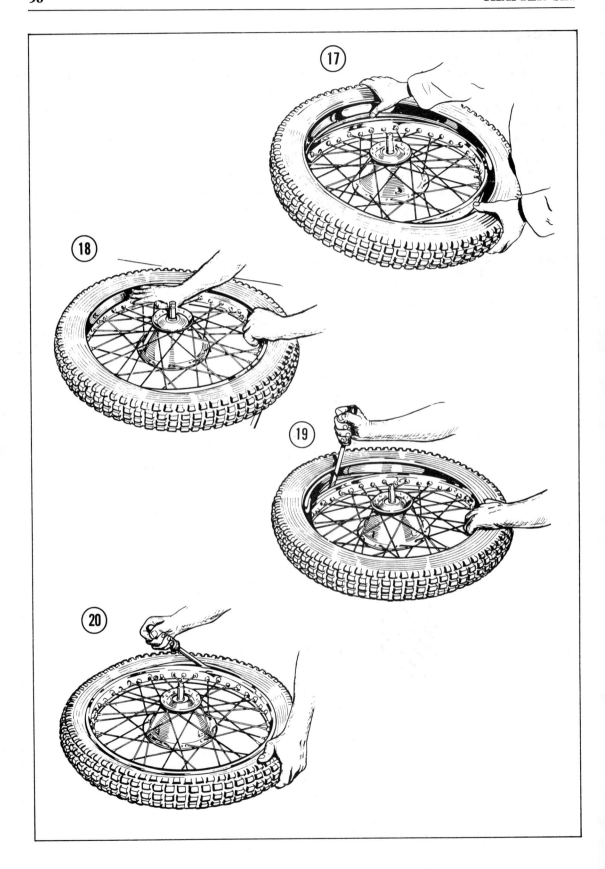

Checking Wheel Runout

1. Support the wheel firmly by the axle in such a way that it is free to rotate.

2. Position a dial indicator as shown in **Figure 21**. A piece of wire, bent to touch the rim at its maximum point of runout, can be used as a substitute for approximate truing.

3. Observe the dial indicator as the wheel is rotated through one complete revolution. Runout for all models should not exceed 0.12 inch (3.0mm).

4. Adjust the spokes until runout is within acceptable limits. The spoke opposite a high point should be adjusted first working around the wheel in either direction.

Brakes

The brake assemblies on all Ducati motorcycles are similar to those shown in **Figure 22 and Figure 23**. These exploded views have been included to help identify components and to speed repair.

1. The brake assemblies will practically fall apart when the axle is removed.

2. Check the brake lining surfaces carefully for scoring, oil residue, or glazing. Glazed lining can be reinstated by roughing the surface with a wire brush.

3. Measure the lining at its thinnest part. Replace both shoes when any part of either lining is worn to less than 1/16 inch (1.5mm).

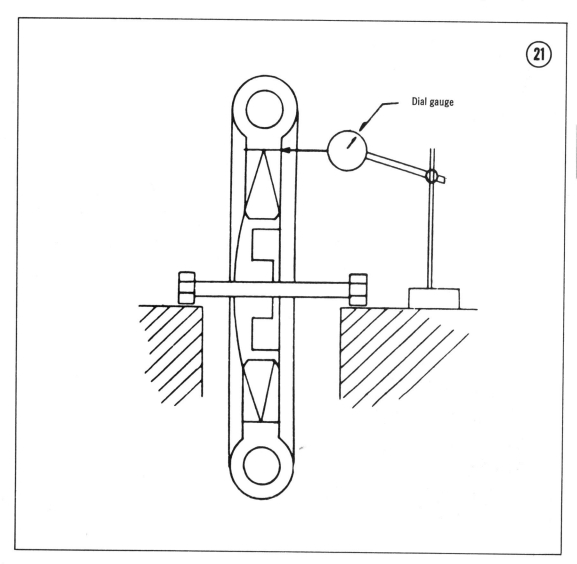

Dial gauge

6

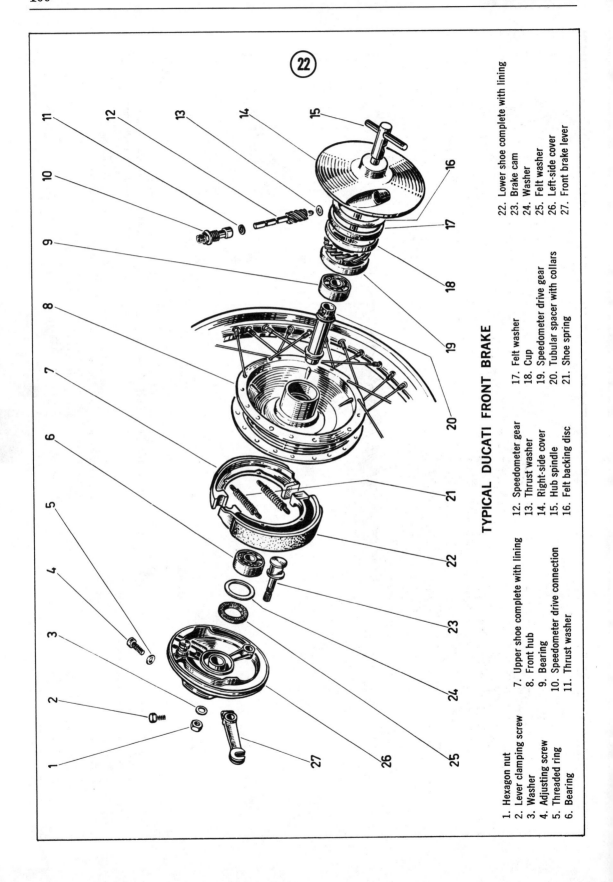

㉒

TYPICAL DUCATI FRONT BRAKE

1. Hexagon nut
2. Lever clamping screw
3. Washer
4. Adjusting screw
5. Threaded ring
6. Bearing

7. Upper shoe complete with lining
8. Front hub
9. Bearing
10. Speedometer drive connection
11. Thrust washer

12. Speedometer gear
13. Thrust washer
14. Right-side cover
15. Hub spindle
16. Felt backing disc

17. Felt washer
18. Cup
19. Speedometer drive gear
20. Tubular spacer with collars
21. Shoe spring

22. Lower shoe complete with lining
23. Brake cam
24. Washer
25. Felt washer
26. Left-side cover
27. Front brake lever

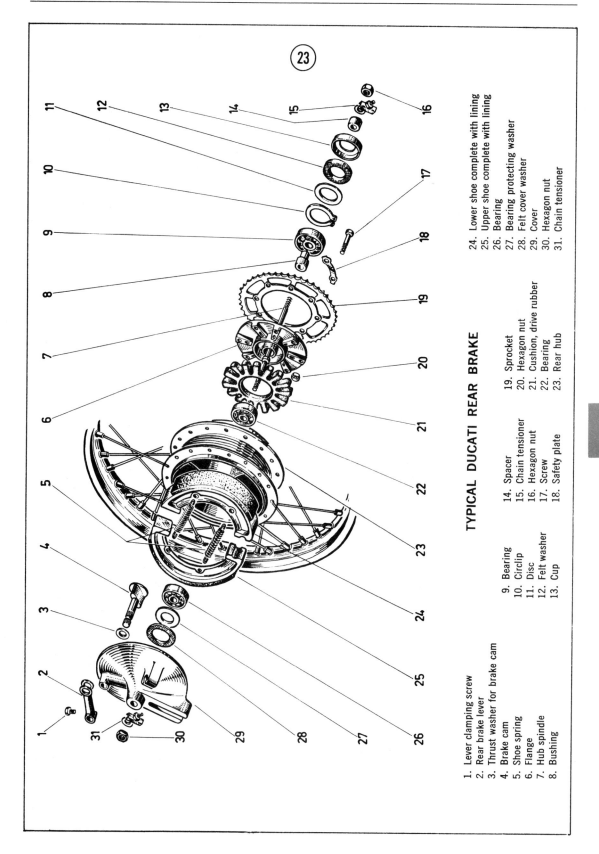

(23)

TYPICAL DUCATI REAR BRAKE

1. Lever clamping screw
2. Rear brake lever
3. Thrust washer for brake cam
4. Brake cam
5. Shoe spring
6. Flange
7. Hub spindle
8. Bushing

9. Bearing
10. Circlip
11. Disc
12. Felt washer
13. Cup

14. Spacer
15. Chain tensioner
16. Hexagon nut
17. Screw
18. Safety plate

19. Sprocket
20. Hexagon nut
21. Cushion, drive rubber
22. Bearing
23. Rear hub

24. Lower shoe complete with lining
25. Upper shoe complete with lining
26. Bearing
27. Bearing protecting washer
28. Felt cover washer
29. Cover
30. Hexagon nut
31. Chain tensioner

6

4. If the return spring is stretched, the shoes will not retract fully and the brakes will drag reducing their efficiency.

5. Apply small quantities of high-temperature grease to the cam lobes. Too much grease may find its way onto the linings.

6. Reinstall the brakes, replace the axle and adjust the cables for optimum efficiency. Allow some free-play in the levers to avoid causing the brakes to drag or lock up.

7. If it's impossible to adjust the brakes at the cable, it may be necessary to move the position of lever on the side of the backing plate. To do so, loosen the securing nut. Slide the lever off of the spindle and reposition to take up some of the slack.

Rear Shock Absorbers

The shock absorbers are a sealed factory unit and cannot be repaired by the average mechanic. It's far simpler and less expensive to replace them if damping efficiency decreases or if the seals appear to be leaking. **Figure 24** shows a typical shock.

The shocks may be adjusted to suit different rider weights as riding conditions. Twist the collar under the spring to increase tension for stiffer suspension. Be sure to adjust each shock equally to evenly distribute the load.

Always replace the shocks in pairs since the springs can gradually weaken with use.

Swinging Arm

The swinging arm, with the shocks mounted, comprises the rear suspension. Shimmy, wander, and wheel hop are common symptoms of worn swing arm bushings. To replace these, proceed as follows.

1. Remove the rear wheel.

2. Remove the pivot shaft and lower shock mounting bolts.

3. Press out the old bushings. This operation may require the help of a professional mechanic.

4. Press in the new bushings. Here, again, you may need the help of a shop.

5. After assembly, check the pivot point for excessive lateral play. Clearance between the

bushings and swing arm shouldn't exceed 0.02 inch (0.5mm).

Drive Chain

The chain is one of the most neglected parts of a motorcycle. It is seldom adjusted properly and only rarely lubricated. Inspect and lubricate the chain periodically. Special foaming lubes are available which can enter and lubricate the inner rollers and are less likely to fly away due to centrifugal force. Try to work out any kinks which may form in the chain links.

Replace the chain if the kinks are too bad to be fixed or if the chain can be moved sideways more than ½ inch when mounted on the bike.

Periodically remove the chain and allow it to sit in a container of motor oil for 24 hours or more. Hang the chain up by one end and allow it to drip dry for several hours. Apply a good quality chain lube and reinstall.

Install the master link so that the clip opening faces opposite to the direction of chain movement (**Figure 25**). Failure to do so may result in the loss of the clip and damage to the chain.

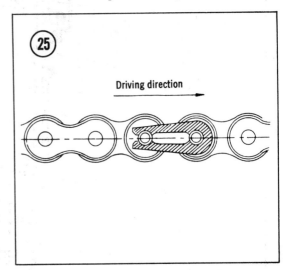

(25)

Driving direction

Exhaust Pipe

Carbon deposits can form in the exhaust pipe and cause a loss in engine efficiency and power. The easiest way to remove these deposits is to run a piece of used drive chain through the pipe. Another method is to chuck a length of wire cable, with one end flared, in an electric drill. Run the wire through the pipe a few times.

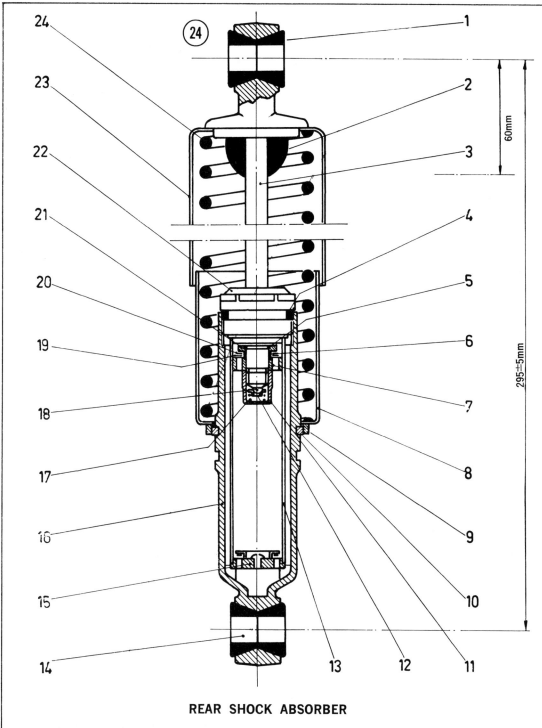

REAR SHOCK ABSORBER

1. Conical shock rubbers	7. Piston	13. Pressure tube	19. Disc valve
2. Bump stop rubber	8. Chrome plated sleeve	14. Conical shock rubbers	20. Disc washer
3. Piston rod	9. Collar for half rings	15. Complete bottom valve	21. Shroud for spring ring
4. External oil ring	10. Half rings	16. Main body	22. Bushing with oil seal
5. Spring washer	11. Piston retaining cap nut	17. Hydraulic shock spring	23. Painted sleeve
6. Piston spacer	12. Ball cup	18. Ball	24. Spring

Rear Sprocket

Check the sprocket for wear or damaged teeth. **Figure 26** shows how a worn gear may appear. Proper lubrication and checking the tightness of the mounting bolts can prolong the life of this part.

Miscellaneous Frame Components

The remaining frame components are either not subject to wear or are too simple in removal and assembly to discuss in detail. Critical segments of the Ducati are explained in detail throughout this book.

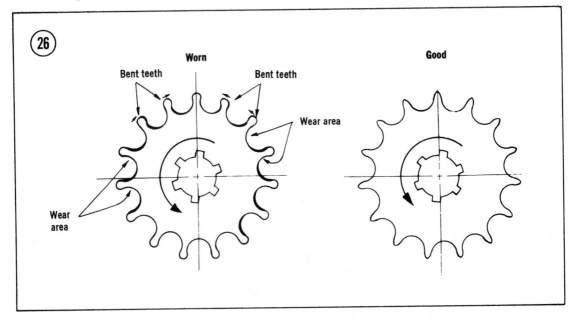

CHAPTER SEVEN

PERIODIC SERVICE AND MAINTENANCE

To gain the utmost in safety, performance, and useful life from your machine, you must make periodic inspections and adjustments. Frequently, minor problems found in such inspections are simple and inexpensive to correct at the time, but could lead to major problems later.

Table 1 is a suggested maintenance schedule. **Table 2** lists lubrication intervals and lubricants. The procedures for performing these services are described in the applicable chapters.

Table 1   SUGGESTED MAINTENANCE

Maintenance Item	Miles thereafter		
	Initial 500	1,000	2,000
Change oil	X		X
Check spark plug	X	X	
Ignition timing	X		X
Adjust clutch	X		X
Adjust carburetor	X		X
Service air cleaner			X
Clean exhaust system			X
Adjust brakes	X	X	
Check air pressure (30-32 lbs.)	X	X	
Clean brakes		X	
Inspect chain	X		X
Check spokes		X	
Tighten all fastenings	X		X
Clean fuel strainer		X	
Remove carbon			X
Check electrical equipment	X	X	
Grease chassis		X	

7

Table 2   LUBRICATION INTERVALS AND LUBRICANTS

Item	Operation	Interval	Lubricant
Engine	Replace the oil in the engine sump, when the engine is hot	After the first 300 miles (500 kms)	Multigrade or racing SAE 40
	Replace the oil in the engine sump, when the engine is hot	After the first 600 miles (1,000 kms)	Multigrade or racing SAE 40
	Maintain oil level	Every 300 miles (500 kms)	Multigrade or racing SAE 40
	Replace the oil, when the engine is hot, and clean filter	Every 1,200 miles (2,000 kms)	Multigrade or racing SAE 40
Lobes of camshaft, gears and bearings	Grease	During assembly	Grease, 30 wt.
Cables for: throttle, front brake, clutch, rear brake & speedometer	Grease	During assembly	Grease, 30 wt.
Speedometer drive	Grease	During assembly and every 1,000 miles (1,500 kms)	Grease, 30 wt.
Lever controls on the handlebar and throttle twist grip control	Grease	During assembly and every 2,000 miles (3,000 kms)	Grease, 30 wt.
Steering boxes	Grease by pressure pump		Grease, 30 wt.
Front fork tubes	Drain fully and fill with new oil. 150cc (5.2 ozs.) for 160 Monza. All others, 110cc (3.5 ozs.)	During assembly or when the fork tubes are of different length	Hydraulic brake fluid or shock absorber oil. Monza uses SAE 20 wt. motor oil.
Outer front fork sliding column, and front suspension spring	Cover with grease	During assembly	Grease, 30 wt.
Brake cams and barrels of brake hub levers	Grease	During assembly and every 1,200 miles (2,000 kms)	Grease, 30 wt.
Starter lever joint	Grease	During assembly and every 2,000 miles (3,000 kms)	Grease, 30 wt.
Rear suspension joint	Grease	During assembly	Grease, 30 wt.
	Lubricate by pressure	Every 1,200 miles (2,000 kms)	Multigrade
Central stand spindle and rear brake pedal spindle	Grease	During assembly and every 1,200 miles (2,000 kms)	Grease, 30 wt.
Chain	Grease	Every 1,200 miles (2,000 kms)	Grease, 30 wt.

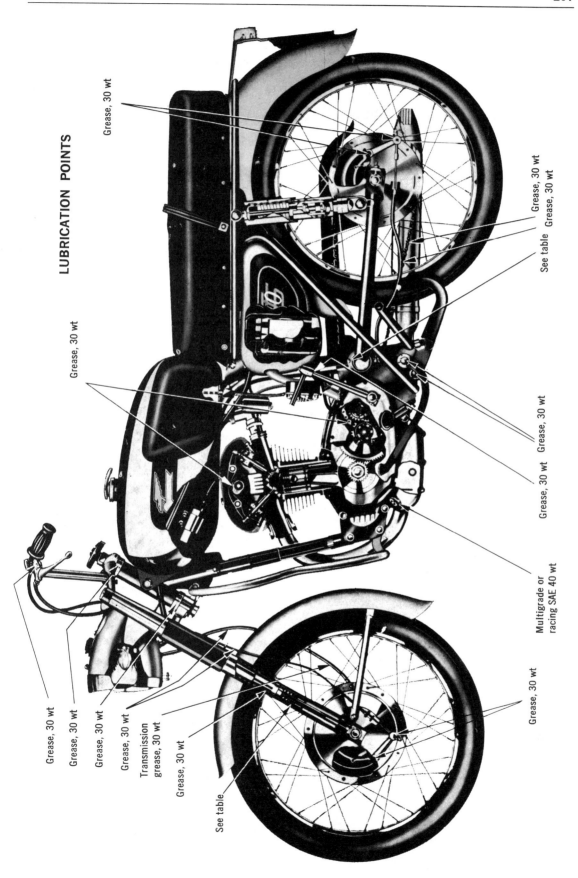

LUBRICATION POINTS

Grease, 30 wt

Grease, 30 wt

Grease, 30 wt
Grease, 30 wt

See table

Grease, 30 wt

Grease, 30 wt Grease, 30 wt

Multigrade or
racing SAE 40 wt

Grease, 30 wt

Grease, 30 wt

Grease, 30 wt

Grease, 30 wt

Grease, 30 wt

Transmission
grease, 30 wt

Grease, 30 wt

See table

7

CHAPTER EIGHT

GUIDE TO TROUBLESHOOTING

Diagnosing motorcycle ills is relatively simple if you use orderly procedures and keep a few basic principles in mind.

Never assume anything. Don't overlook the obvious. If you are riding along and the bike suddenly quits, check the easiest, most accessible problem spots first. Is there gasoline in the tank? Is the gas petcock in the "on" or "reserve" position? Has a spark plug wire fallen off? Check the ignition switch. Sometimes the weight of keys on a key ring may turn the ignition off suddenly.

If nothing obvious turns up in a cursory check, look a little further. Learning to recognize and describe symptoms will make repairs easier for you or a mechanic at the shop. Describe problems accurately and fully. Saying that "it won't run" isn't the same as saying "it quit on the highway at high speed and wouldn't start," or that "it sat in my garage for three months and then wouldn't start."

Gather as many symptoms together as possible to aid in diagnosis. Note whether the engine lost power gradually or all at once, what color smoke (if any) came from the exhausts and so on. Remember that the more complicated a machine is, the easier it is to troubleshoot because symptoms point to specific problems.

You don't need fancy equipment or complicated test gear to determine whether repairs can be attempted at home. A few simple checks could save a large repair bill and time lost while the bike sits in a dealer's service department. On the other hand, be realistic and don't attempt repairs beyond your abilities. Service departments tend to charge heavily for putting together a disassembled engine that may have been abused. Some won't even take on such a job—so use common sense and don't get in over your head.

OPERATING REQUIREMENTS

An engine needs three basics to run properly: correct gas-air mixture, compression, and a spark at the right time. If one or more are missing, the engine won't run. The electrical system is the weakest link of the three. More problems result from electrical breakdowns than from any other source. Keep that in mind before you begin tampering with carburetor adjustments and the like.

If a bike has been sitting for any length of time and refuses to start, check the battery for a charged condition first and then look to the gasoline delivery system. This includes the tank, fuel petcocks, lines and the carburetor. Rust may have formed in the tank, obstructing fuel flow. Gasoline deposits may have gummed up carburetor jets and air passages. Gasoline tends to lose its potency after standing for long periods. Condensation may contaminate it with water. Drain old gas and try starting with a fresh tankful.

Compression or the lack of it, usually enters the picture only in the case of older machines. Worn or broken pistons, rings and cylinder bores could prevent starting. Generally a gradual power loss and harder and harder starting will be readily apparent in this case.

WHAT TO DO
IF THE ENGINE WON'T START

Check gas flow first. Remove the gas cap and look into the tank. If gas is present, pull off a fuel line at the carburetor and see if gas flows freely. If none comes out, the fuel tap may be shut off, blocked by rust or foreign matter or the fuel line may be stopped up or kinked. If the carburetor is getting usable fuel, turn to the electrical system next.

Check that the battery is charged by turning on the lights or by beeping the horn. Refer to your owner's manual for starting procedures with a dead battery. Have the battery recharged if necessary.

Pull off a spark plug cap, remove the spark plug and reconnect the cap. Lay the plug against the cylinder head so its base makes a good connection and turn the engine over with the kickstarter. A fat, blue spark should jump across the electrodes. If there is no spark, or a weak one, there is electrical system trouble. Check for a defective plug by replacing it with a known good one. Don't assume a plug is good just because it's new.

Once the plug has been cleared of guilt, but there's still no spark, start backtracking through the system. If the contact at the end of the spark plug wire can be exposed it can be held about ⅛ inch from the head while the engine is turned over to check for a spark. Remember to hold the wire only by its insulation to avoid a nasty shock. If the plug wires are dirty, greasy, or wet, wrap a rag around them so you won't get shocked. If you do feel a shock or see sparks along the wire, clean or replace the wire and/or its connections.

If there's no spark at the plug wire, look for loose connections at the coil and battery. If all seems in order here, check next for oily or dirty contact points. Clean points with electrical contact cleaner or a strip of paper. With the ignition switch turned on, open and close the points manually with a screwdriver.

No spark at the points with this test indicates a failure in the ignition system. Refer to the *Electrical Service* section in this manual for checkout procedures for the entire system and individual components.

Note that a spark plug of the incorrect heat range (too cold) may cause hard starting. Set gap to specification. If you have just ridden through a puddle or washed the bike and it won't start, dry off the plug and plug wire. Water may have entered the carburetor and fouled the fuel under these conditions, but a wet plug and wire is the more likely problem.

If a healthy spark occurs at the right time, and there is adequate gas flow **to** the carburetor, check the carburetor itself at this time. Make sure all jets and air passages are clean. Check float level and adjust if necessary. Shake the float to check for gasoline inside it and replace or repair as indicated. Check that the carburetor is mounted snugly and no air is leaking past the manifold. Check for a clogged air filter.

Compression may be checked in the field by turning the kickstarter by hand and noting that an adequate resistance is felt or by removing a spark plug and placing a finger over the plug hole and feeling for pressure. Use a compression gauge if possible. Compression should generally read 150 lbs. per square inch or more.

Valve adjustments should be checked next. Sticking, burned or broken valves may hamper starting. As a last resort, check valve timing as described in the *Engine Service* section.

8

POOR IDLING

Poor idling may be caused by incorrect carburetor adjustment, incorrect timing, ignition system defects, an intake manifold leak or leakage between the carburetors at the balance tube. Check the gas cap vent for an obstruction.

MISFIRING

Misfiiring can be caused by a weak spark or dirty plug. Check for fuel contamination. Run the machine at night or in a darkened garage to check for spark leaks along the plug wire and under the spark plug cap. If misfiring occurs only at certain throttle settings, refer to the carburetor service section for the specfic carburetor circuits involved. Misfiring under heavy load as when climbing hills or accelerating is usually caused by a bad spark plug.

FLAT SPOT

If the engine seems to die momentarily when the throttle is opened and then recovers, check for a dirty main jet in the carburetor, water in the fuel or an excessively lean mixture.

LACK OF POWER

Poor condition of rings, piston or cylinder will cause a lack of power and speed. Check that valves are correctly adjusted. Ignition timing should be checked along with the automatic spark advance.

OVERHEATING

If the engine seems to run too hot all the time, be sure you are not idling it for long periods. Air cooled engines are not designed to operate at a standstill for any length of time. Heavy stop and go traffic is hard on a motorcycle engine. Spark plugs of the wrong heat range can burn pistons. An excessively lean gas mixture may cause overheating. Check ignition timing. Don't ride in too high a gear. Broken or worn rings and valves may permit compression gases to leak past them, heating the head and cylinder excessively. Check oil level and use the proper grade lubricants.

BACKFIRING

Check that the timing is not advanced too far. Check the automatic advance mechanism for broken or sticking parts. Check fuel for contamination.

ENGINE NOISES

Experience is needed to diagnose accurately in this area. Noises are hard to differentiate and harder yet to describe. Deep knocking noises usually mean main bearing failure. A slapping noise generally comes from a loose piston. A light knocking noise during acceleration may be a bad connecting rod bearing. Pinging, which sounds like marbles being shaken in a tin can, is caused by ignition advanced too far or gasoline with too low an octane rating. Pinging should be corrected immediately or damage to the piston will result. Compression leaks at the head cylinder joint will sound like a rapid on and off squeal.

PISTON SEIZURE

Piston seizure is caused by incorrect piston clearances when fitted, fitting rings with improper end gap, too thin an oil being used, incorrect spark plug heat range or incorrect ignition timing. Overheating from any cause may result in seizure.

VIBRATION

Excessive vibration may be caused by loose motor mounts, worn engine or transmission bearings, loose wheels, worn swinging arm bushings, a generally poor running engine, broken or cracked frame or one that has been damaged in a collision.

HIGH OIL CONSUMPTION

High oil consumption and loss of compression often go hand in hand. Check condition of rings, piston, cylinder and valves. Worn valve stems or valve guides may be at fault. Use the correct grade of oil.

CLUTCH SLIP OR DRAG

Clutch slip may be due to worn plates, improper adjustment or glazed plates. A dragging clutch could result from damaged or bent plates, improper adjustment or even clutch spring pressure.

TRANSMISSION PROBLEMS

A grinding when shifting may be a result of worn synchronizers on the transmission gears or a sticking or non-disengaging clutch. Bent or broken teeth may cause hard shifting. A bent shifting rod or mainshaft or layshaft could cause hard shifting. Popping out of gear could be due to worn dogs on the gears or misadjustment in the shifting mechanism.

POOR HANDLING

Poor handling may be caused by improper tire pressures, a damaged frame or swinging arm, worn shocks or front forks, weak fork springs, a bent or broken steering stem, misaligned wheels, loose or missing spokes, worn tires, bent handlebars, worn wheel bearings or dragging brakes.

BRAKE SYSTEM

Sticking brakes may be caused by broken or weak return springs, improper cable or rod adjustment or dry pivot and cam bushings. Grabbing brakes may be caused by greasy linings which must be replaced. Brake grab may also be due to out of round drums or linings which have broken loose from the shoes. Glazed linings or brake pads will cause loss of stopping power.

LIGHTING SYSTEM

Bulbs which continuously burn out may be caused by excessive vibration, loose connections that permit sudden current surges, poor battery connections or installation of wrong type bulb.

A dead battery or one which discharges quickly may be caused by a faulty generator or rectifier. Check for loose or corroded terminals. Shorted battery cells or broken terminals will keep a battery from charging. Low water level will decrease a battery's capacity. A battery left uncharged after installation will sulphate, rendering it useless.

A majority of light and horn or other electrical accessory problems are caused by loose or corroded ground connections. Check those first and then substitute known good units for easier troubleshooting.

8

CHAPTER NINE

SPECIFICATIONS

This chapter contains specifications and performance figures for the various Ducati models covered by this book. The tables are arranged in order of increasing engine size. Since there are differences between various models of the same engine size, be sure to consult the correct table for the motorcycle in question.

SPECIFICATIONS — 160 MONZA JR.

Overall length	79.9 inches	Maximum rpm	8,000
Overall height	36.6 inches	Carburetion	Dell'Orto, UB 22 BS, 22mm
Wheelbase	52.3 inches	Lubrication	Wet sump
Weight	233.7 lbs.	Ignition	Coil, battery
Engine type	Single cylinder, inclined 10°, four-stroke, overhead cam	Electrical equipment	Full street lighting
		Transmission	Four-speed, constant mesh
Maximum speed	63 mph	Frame type	Single downtube, engine in unit
Fuel consumption	84 mpg		
Bore and stroke	61 x 52mm	Front suspension	Telehydraulic fork
Displacement	156cc	Rear suspension	Swing arm, shock
Compression ratio	8.2 : 1	Wheels and tires	2.75 x 16 front, 3.25 x 16 rear

SPECIFICATIONS — 250 MONZA

Overall length	78.7 inches	Maximum rpm	7,200
Overall height	42.1 inches	Carburetion	Dell'Orto, UBF 24 BS, 24mm
Wheelbase	51.9 inches	Lubrication	Wet sump
Weight	275.6 lbs.	Ignition	Coil, battery
Engine type	Single cylinder, inclined 10°,	Electrical equipment	Full street lighting
	four-stroke, overhead cam	Transmission	Five-speed, constant mesh
Maximum speed	80 mph	Frame type	Single downtube, engine
Fuel consumption	73 mpg		in unit
Bore and stroke	74 x 57.8mm	Front suspension	Telehydraulic fork
Displacement	248.6cc	Rear suspension	Swing arm, shock
Compression ratio	8.0 : 1	Wheels and tires	2.75 x 18 front, 3.00 x 18 rear

SPECIFICATIONS — 250 GT

Overall length	78.7 inches	Maximum rpm	7,200
Overall height	42.1 inches	Carburetion	Dell'Orto, UBF 24 BS, 24mm
Wheelbase	51.9 inches	Lubrication	Wet sump
Weight	275.6 lbs.	Ignition	Coil, battery
Engine type	Single cylinder, inclined 10°,	Electrical equipment	Full street lighting
	four-stroke, overhead cam	Transmission	Five-speed, constant mesh
Maximum speed	105 mph	Frame type	Single downtube, engine
Fuel consumption	72 mpg		in unit
Bore and stroke	74 x 57.8mm	Front suspension	Telehydraulic fork
Displacement	248.6	Rear suspension	Swing arm, shock
Compression ratio	8.0 : 1	Wheels and tires	2.75 x 18 front, 3.00 x 18 rear

SPECIFICATIONS — 250 MARK 3

Overall length	78.7 inches	Maximum rpm	8,000
Overall height	42.9 inches	Carburetion	Dell'Orto, SSI 27 A, 27mm
Wheelbase	51.9 inches	Lubrication	Wet sump
Weight	242.5 lbs.	Ignition	Coil, magneto
Engine type	Single cylinder, inclined 10°,	Electrical equipment	Full street lighting
	four-stroke, overhead cam	Transmission	Five-speed, constant mesh
Maximum speed	110 mph	Frame type	Single downtube, engine
Fuel consumption	68 mpg		in unit
Bore and stroke	74 x 57.8mm	Front suspension	Telehydraulic fork
Displacement	248.5cc	Rear suspension	Swing arm, shock
Compression ratio	10.1 : 1	Wheels and tires	2.50 x 18 front, 2.75 x 18 rear

9

SPECIFICATIONS — 250 MACH I

Overall length	78.7 inches	Maximum rpm	8,500
Overall height	29.9 inches	Carburetion	Dell'Orto, SSI 29 D, 29mm
Wheelbase	53.1 inches	Lubrication	Wet sump
Weight	255.7 lbs.	Ignition	Coil, battery
Engine type	Single cylinder, inclined 10°,	Electrical equipment	Full street lighting
	four-stroke, overhead cam	Transmission	Five-speed, constant mesh
Maximum speed	106 mph	Frame type	Single downtube, engine
Fuel consumption	60 mpg		in unit
Bore and stroke	74 x 57.8mm	Front suspension	Telehydraulic fork
Displacement	248.5cc	Rear suspension	Swing arm, shock
Compression ratio	10.0 : 1	Wheels and tires	2.50 x 18 front, 2.75 x 18 rear

SPECIFICATIONS — 250 MOTOCROSS (SCRAMBLER)

Overall length	79.5 inches	Maximum rpm	8,000
Overall height	41.3 inches	Carburetion	Dell'Orto, SSI 27 A, 27mm
Wheelbase	53.1 inches	Lubrication	Wet sump
Weight	264.5 lbs.	Ignition	Coil, magneto
Engine type	Single cylinder, inclined 10°,	Electrical equipment	Full street lighting
	four-stroke, overhead cam	Transmission	Five-speed, constant mesh
Maximum speed	No claim	Frame type	Single downtube, engine
Fuel consumption	68 mpg		in unit
Bore and stroke	74 x 57.8mm	Front suspension	Telehydraulic fork
Displacement	248.5cc	Rear suspension	Swing arm, shock
Compression ratio	9.2 : 1	Wheels and tires	3.50 x 19 front, 4.00 x 18 rear

SPECIFICATIONS 350 SEBRING

Overall length	78.7 inches	Maximum rpm	6,250
Overall height	42.1 inches	Carburetion	Dell'Orto, UBF 24 BS
Wheelbase	52.3 inches	Lubrication	Wet sump
Weight	271.1 lbs.	Ignition	Coil, battery
Engine type	Single cylinder, inclined 10°,	Electrical equipment	Full street lighting
	four-stroke, overhead cam	Transmission	Five-speed, constant mesh
Maximum speed	78 mph	Frame type	Single downtube, engine
Fuel consumption	52 mpg		in unit
Bore and stroke	76 x 75mm	Front suspension	Telehydraulic fork
Displacement	340.2cc	Rear suspension	Swing arm, shock
Compression ratio	8.5 : 1	Wheels and tires	2.75 x 18 front, 3.00 x 18 rear

SPECIFICATIONS — 450 MARK 3 AND MARK 3 D

Overall length	78.7 inches	Maximum rpm	8,000
Overall height	37.0 inches	Carburetion	Dell'Orto, VHB 29 A, 29mm
Wheelbase	53.5 inches	Lubrication	Wet sump
Weight	287 lbs.	Ignition	Coil, battery
Engine type	Single cylinder, inclined 10°, four-stroke, overhead cam	Electrical equipment	Full street lighting
		Transmission	Five-speed, constant mesh
Maximum speed	No claim	Frame type	Single downtube, engine
Fuel consumption	No claim		in unit
Bore and stroke	86 x 75mm	Front suspension	Telehydraulic fork
Displacement	435.7cc	Rear suspension	Swing arm, shock
Compression ratio	9.3 : 1	Wheels and tires	3.00 x 18 front, 3.25 x 18 rear

SPECIFICATIONS — 450 SCRAMBLER

Overall length	83.5 inches	Maximum rpm	8,000
Overall height	45.3 inches	Carburetion	Dell'Orto, VHB 29 A, 29mm
Wheelbase	54.3 inches	Lubrication	Wet sump
Weight	293 lbs.	Ignition	Coil, battery
Engine type	Single cylinder, inclined 10°, four-stroke, overhead cam	Electrical equipment	Full street lighting
		Transmission	Five-speed, constant mesh
Maximum speed	No claim	Frame type	Single downtube, engine
Fuel consumption	No claim		in unit
Bore and stroke	86 x 75mm	Front suspension	Telehydraulic fork
Displacement	435.7cc	Rear suspension	Swing arm, shock
Compression ratio	9.3 : 1	Wheels and tires	3.50 x 19 front, 4.00 x 18 rear

SPECIFICATIONS — 450 DESMO-CROSS-SPECIAL

Overall length	85.8 inches	Maximum rpm	8,500
Overall height	47.2 inches	Carburetion	Dell'Orto VHB 29 A, 29mm
Wheelbase	46.3 inches	Lubrication	Wet sump
Weight	274 lbs.	Ignition	Magneto
Engine type	Single cylinder, inclined 10°, four-stroke, overhead cam	Electrical equipment	None
		Transmission	Five-speed, constant mesh
Maximum speed	No claim	Frame type	Single downtube, engine
Fuel consumption	No claim		in unit
Bore and stroke	86 x 75mm	Front suspension	Telehydraulic fork
Displacement	435.7cc	Rear suspension	Swing arm, shock
Compression ratio	10.0 : 1	Wheels and tires	3.50 x 19 front, 4.00 x 18 rear

9

CHAPTER TEN

USEFUL FORMULAS AND TABLES

It is often necessary to convert metric to American dimensions or vice versa. This chapter contains formulas for doing so, with typical examples worked out. Also in this chapter are other useful tables and formulas.

CONVERSIONS

Multiply	by	To obtain
Volume		
Cubic centimeters	0.061	Cubic inches
Cubic inches	16.387	Cubic centimeters
Liters	0.264	Gallons
Gallons	3.785	Liters
Liters	1.057	Quarts
Quarts	0.946	Liters
Cubic centimeters	0.0339	Fluid ounces
Fluid ounces	29.57	Cubic centimeters
Length		
Millimeters	0.03937	Inches
Inches	25.4	Millimeters
Centimeters	0.3937	Inches
Inches	2.54	Centimeters
Kilometers	0.6214	Miles
Miles	1.609	Kilometers
Meters	3.281	Feet
Feet	0.3048	Meters
Millimeters	0.10	Centimeters
Centimeters	10.0	Millimeters
Weight		
Kilograms	2.205	Pounds
Pounds	0.4536	Kilograms
Grams	0.03527	Ounces
Ounces	28.35	Grams
Other		
Metric horsepower	1.014	Brake horsepower
Brake horsepower	0.9859	Metric horsepower
Kilogram-meters	7.235	Foot-pounds
Foot-pounds	0.1383	Kilogram-meters
Kilometers per liter	2.352	Miles per gallon
Miles per gallon	0.4252	Kilometers per liter
Square millimeters	0.00155	Square inches
Square inches	645.2	Square millimeters
Square inches	6.452	Square centimeters
Square centimeters	0.155	Square inches
Kilometers per hour	0.6214	Miles per hour
Miles per hour	1.609	Kilometers per hour
Foot-pounds	0.1383	Kilogram-meters
Kilogram-meters	7.233	Foot-pounds
Pounds per square inch	0.0703	Kilograms per square centimeter
Kilograms per square centimeter	14.22	Pounds per square inch
Miles per hour	88	Feet per minute
Feet per minute	0.01136	Miles per hour
Miles per hour	1.467	Feet per second

10

EXAMPLES OF CONVERSIONS

1. To convert 250 cubic centimeters to cubic inches, multiply 250 cubic centimeters by 0.061:

$$250 \times 0.061 = 15.25 \text{ cubic inches}$$

2. To convert 0.65 inch to millimeters, multiply 0.65 inch by 25.4:

$$0.65 \times 25.4 = 16.51 \text{ millimeters}$$

3. To convert 76 kilograms to pounds, multiply 76 kilograms by 2.205:

$$76 \times 2.205 = 167.58 \text{ pounds}$$

4. To convert 41 miles per gallon to kilometers per liter, multiply 41 miles per gallon by 0.4252:

$$41 \times 0.4252 = 17.43 \text{ kilometers per liter}$$

5. To convert 50 miles per hour to feet per second, multiply 50 miles per hour by 1.467:

$$50 \times 1.467 = 73.35 \text{ feet per second}$$

TEMPERATURE

It is sometimes specified in a service manual to perform a repair operation at a certain temperature, such as heating crankcase halves to 150 degrees C before installing bearings. There are two basic formulas for converting degrees F to degrees C and vice versa:

$$C = 5/9 \ (F - 32)$$
$$F = 9/5C + 32$$

Example 1

Measurement temperature for the electrolyte in a battery is specified as 68 degrees F. What is that temperature in degrees C?

$$C = 5/9 \ (F - 32)$$
$$= 5/9 \ (68 - 32)$$
$$= 5/9 \times 36$$
$$= \frac{180}{9}$$
$$= 20 \text{ degrees C}$$

Example 2

A motorcycle service manual specifies that main bearings be heated to 200 degrees C before installing them onto the crankshaft. What is that temperature in degrees F?

$$F = 9/5 \ C + 32$$
$$= (9/5 \times 200) + 32$$
$$= 360 + 32$$
$$= 392 \text{ degrees F}$$

PISTON DISPLACEMENT

The formula for finding piston displacement can be expressed as:

$$D = \pi \times R^2 \times S \times N$$

D = Piston displacement

π = 3.1416 (a constant)

S = Piston stroke

N = Number of cylinders

R = Radius of one cylinder (one-half of bore)

(R^2, read "R squared", means R multiplied by itself)

Example 1

A single cylinder engine has a bore of 70 millimeters, and a stroke of 62 millimeters. What is its displacement?

First convert 70 millimeters (bore) and 62 millimeters (stroke) to centimeters by dividing each by 10, which is equivalent to multiplying each by 0.10. This step is necessary so that our answer will come out in cubic centimeters. Then using bore and stroke figures expressed in *centimeters* in the formula:

$$R = \text{one-half of bore} = 3.5$$
$$S = 6.2$$
$$N = 1$$
$$D = \pi \times R^2 \times S \times N$$
$$= 3.1416 \times (3.5)^2 \times 6.2 \times 1$$
$$= 3.1416 \times 12.25 \times 6.2$$
$$= 238.6 \text{ cubic centimeters}$$

Example 2

A 3-cylinder engine has a bore of 60 milli-meters and a stroke of 58.8 millimeters. What is its piston displacement?

First convert both bore and stroke into centi-meters by multiplying by 0.10:

R = one-half of bore = 3 centimeters

S = 5.88 centimeters

N = 3

$$D = \pi \times R^2 \times S \times N$$

$$= 3.1416 \times (3.0)^2 \times 5.88 \times 3$$

$$= 3.1416 \times 9 \times 5.88 \times 3$$

$$= 498.75 \text{ cubic centimeters}$$

Note that the formula will work equally well if bore and stroke are expressed in inches or millimeters. If they are expressed in inches, the answer will come out in cubic inches. The answer will come out in cubic millimeters if millimeters are used in the formula.

COMPRESSION RATIO

To determine compression ratio of an engine, it is first necessary to know piston displacement (of one cylinder) and combustion chamber vol-ume. The formula can be expressed as:

Compression ratio =

$$\frac{\text{Piston displacement} + \text{Combustion chamber vol.}}{\text{Combustion chamber volume}}$$

Example

An engine has a piston displacement of 244.6 cubic centimeters and a combustion chamber volume of 41.5 cubic centimeters. What is its compression ratio?

$$\text{Compression ratio} = \frac{244.6 + 38.2}{38.2}$$

$$= \frac{282.8}{38.2}$$

$$= 7.4 \text{ to 1 (rounded off)}$$

HORSEPOWER AND TORQUE

There is sometimes confusion about horse-power and torque. Horsepower is a measure of how much work can be done in a given length of time. One horsepower is equal to the work done when a weight of 550 pounds is lifted one foot in one second, or 33,000 pounds lifted one foot in one minute. Torque is merely twisting force de-veloped by an engine, and is not indicative of how much work can be done, unless engine speed is known. The relationship between horse-power, torque, and engine speed can be ex-pressed as:

$$\text{Horsepower} = \frac{\text{rpm} \times \text{Torque}}{5,252}$$

Example 1

A motorcycle engine develops 30 foot-pounds at 6,000 RPM. How much horsepower does it produce at that speed?

$$= \frac{6,000 \times 30}{5,252}$$

$$= \frac{180,000}{5,252}$$

$$= 34.3 \text{ foot-pounds (rounded off)}$$

It is sometimes desired to know how much torque is developed by an engine when horse-power and rpm are known. The formula can then be written as:

$$\text{Torque} = \frac{\text{Horsepower} \times 5,252}{\text{rpm}}$$

Example 2

During a dynamometer test, an engine de-veloped 14.7 horsepower at 3,500 rpm. How much torque did it produce?

$$= \frac{14.7 \times 5,252}{3,500}$$

$$= \frac{77,204}{3,500}$$

$$= 22.06 \text{ foot-pounds (rounded off)}$$

10

PISTON SPEED

It is at times desirable to know the maximum speed pistons reach as they move in their cylinders. This peak speed is reached when the piston is midway between top dead center and bottom dead center. The formula for finding piston speed is:

$$\text{Piston speed} = \frac{\text{Stroke length (in inches)} \times 2 \times \text{rpm}}{12}$$

Example

An engine has a stroke of 2.5 inches. What is its piston speed at 5,000 rpm?

$$\text{Piston speed} = \frac{2.5 \times 2 \times 5,000}{12}$$

$$= \frac{25,000}{12}$$

$$= 2,083 \text{ feet per minute}$$

GEAR RATIO

Gear ratio is defined as the number of revolutions a driving gear makes to turn a driven gear through one complete revolution. By convention, a 4 to 1 gear ratio is said to be lower than a 2.5 to 1 ratio. Note that it is possible to have a gear ratio of less than unity. For a pair of gears, the ratio is found by dividing the number of teeth on the driven gear by the number of teeth on the driving gear.

Example 1

There are 27 teeth on the primary drive gear on a certain motorcycle, and 60 teeth on the primary driven gear. What is its primary reduction ratio?

$$\text{Gear ratio} = \frac{\text{Teeth on driven gear}}{\text{Teeth on driving gear}}$$

$$= \frac{60}{27}$$

$$= 2.22 \text{ to 1 (rounded off)}$$

Example 2

In a certain transmission, there are 27 teeth on 5th input (driving) gear, and 26 teeth on 5th output (driven) gear. What is the gear ratio?

The same formula works equally well for engine and rear wheel sprockets.

$$\text{Gear ratio} = \frac{\text{Teeth on driving gear}}{\text{Teeth on driven gear}}$$

$$= \frac{27}{26}$$

$$= 0.96 \text{ to 1 (rounded off)}$$

Example 3

There are 15 teeth on the engine sprocket on a certain bike, and 49 teeth on the rear wheel sprocket. What is the final reduction ratio?

$$\text{Reduction ratio} = \frac{\text{Number of teeth on driven sprocket}}{\text{Number of teeth on drive sprocket}}$$

$$= \frac{49}{15}$$

$$= 3.27 \text{ to 1 (rounded off)}$$

BOLT TORQUE

The table on the following page lists nominal tightening torque for various metric thread sizes:

BOLT TIGHTENING TORQUES

Diameter (Millimeters)	Pitch (Millimeters)	Torque Foot-pounds	(Meter-kilograms)
Coarse thread			
5	0.90	2.53-3.47	(0.35-0.48)
6	1.00	4.56-6.37	(0.63-0.88)
8	1.25	11.6-15.9	(1.6-2.2)
10	1.50	22.4-30.4	(3.1-4.2)
12	1.75	39.1-54.2	(5.4-7.5)
14	2.00	60.0-83.2	(8.3-11.5)
16	2.00	94.0-130	(13-18)
18	2.50	130-181	(18-25)
20	2.50	188-253	(26-35)
Fine thread			
5	0.50	2.53-3.47	(0.35-0.48)
6	0.75	3.98-5.57	(0.55-0.77)
8	1.00	9.76-13.4	(1.35-1.85)
10	1.25	18.4-25.3	(2.55-3.5)
12	1.50	32.5-44.8	(4.5-6.2)
14	1.50	53.5-73.8	(7.4-10.2)
16	1.50	83.2-116	(11.5-16)
18	1.50	123-166	(17-23)
20	1.50	166-239	(23-33)

10

INDEX

11

MAINTENANCE LOG

DATE	TYPE OF SERVICE	COST	REMARKS

NOTES